Book Five

Program Authors

**Linda Ward Beech • James Beers • Jo Ann Dauzat
Sam V. Dauzat • Tara McCarthy**

Program Consultants

Myra K. Baum
Office of Adult and
   Continuing Education
Brooklyn, New York

Francis J. Feltman, Jr.
Racine Youth Offender
   Correctional Facility
Racine, Wisconsin

Mary Ann Guilliams
Gary Job Corps
San Marcos, Texas

Julie Jacobs
Inmate Literacy Project
Santa Clara County Library
Milpitas, California

Maxine L. McCormick
Workforce Education
Orange County Public Schools
Orlando, Florida

Sandra S. Owens
Laurens County Literacy Council
Laurens, South Carolina

STECK-VAUGHN
ELEMENTARY · SECONDARY · ADULT · LIBRARY

A Harcourt Company

www.steck-vaughn.com

Acknowledgments

Staff Credits

Executive Editor: Ellen Northcutt

Senior Editor: Donna Townsend

Associate Design Director: Joyce Spicer

Supervising Designer: Pamela Heaney

Designer: Jessica Bristow

Production Coordinator: Rebecca Gonzales

Electronic Production Artist: Julia Miracle-Hagaman

Senior Technical Advisor: Alan Klemp

Electronic Production Specialist: Dina Bahan

Photography Credits

Cover (woman painting) Tomás Ovalle; (man & woman) Ken Walker; (woman sitting) Park Street; (woman frowning) Ken Lax; pp.2, 10 Tomás Ovalle; pp.18, 26 Ken Lax; p.34 AP/Wide World Photos; p.42 Courtesy Hoedown; p.43 ©Alain Benanious/Liaison Agency, Inc.; pp.50, 58 Park Street; pp.66, 74 Ken Lax; p.75 (t) ©Bettmann/Corbis; p.75 (b) ©Richard T. Nowitz/Photo Researchers; pp.82, 83, 90-91, 92 Park Street; pp.98, 107 Ken Walker.

Literary Credits

"Ode to Mi Gato," from *Neighborhood Odes* by Gary Soto. Copyright © 1992 by Gary Soto. Reprinted by permission of Harcourt, Inc.

ISBN 07398-2843-6

Contents

Unit 5

Reaching Your Potential

Unit 6

Following Immigration Procedures

Unit 7

Handling Social Relationships

To the Learner

In this book, you will read interesting stories, learn new words, and develop your reading skills. The book has seven units. Each unit has a story about a different topic. As you read the stories, you will review words you already know and learn new words. You will also learn and practice a writing skill, a reading comprehension skill, and a life skill. Then you will have a review to check all the skills you have learned in the unit before you move on to the next unit.

After you have completed all seven units, there is a Final Review that gives you a chance to check all the skills you have learned in the book.

In the At Your Leisure section at the end of the book, you will have a chance to read just for fun. This section has a poem and another reading selection for you to enjoy.

Have a good time using this book. It is written for you!

Instructor's Notes: Read this page to students. Discuss having students keep a notebook or journal of words and original sentences they write. Refer to the *Reading for Today Instructor's Guide* for lesson plans, optional teaching activities, and a discussion of how to use the Learner Placement Form on the inside back cover of this book.

Unit 1   *Finding Work*

Discussion

Remember
Look at the picture. What do you think is happening? Has this ever happened to you or to someone you know?

Predict
Look at the picture and the story title. What do you think this story is about?

You Never Know

April put the pink slip in her wallet. Her hand was shaking. Why was she surprised? People had been talking about the problems at the company for days. They said things weren't good. The company was in trouble and might not make it. April needed this job because she was responsible for her family. Now she would have to find a new job—soon. But where would she find one?

The story continues.

Instructor's Notes: Read the discussion questions with students. Discuss the story title and the situation in the picture. Have students read silently. Have them underline words they don't recognize. Review the underlined words. Have students identify the character.

Review Words

A. Check the words you know.

☐ 1. because   ☐ 2. how   ☐ 3. company

☐ 4. her   ☐ 5. around   ☐ 6. days

☐ 7. after   ☐ 8. other   ☐ 9. responsible

☐ 10. find   ☐ 11. family   ☐ 12. new

B. Read and write the sentences. Circle the review words.

1. The company had to let April and the other workers go.

   _____

   _____

2. How many days will it be before she can find a new job?

   _____

   _____

3. She will look around for work because she is responsible for her family.

   _____

   _____

C. Draw a line to match the word with its opposite. Write the word.

1. **after**   The opposite of <u>old</u> is _____ .

2. **find**   The opposite of <u>night</u> is _____ .

3. **her**   The opposite of <u>before</u> is _____ after _____ .

4. **day**   The opposite of <u>lose</u> is _____ .

5. **new**   The opposite of <u>him</u> is _____ .

Instructor's Notes: Read each set of directions with students. For A, have students read the words aloud and then check known words. Have students practice any unknown words in a notebook or journal.

Sight Words

decided ● fast

possible ● business

A. Read the words above. Then read the sentences.

April **decided** to get a new job as **fast** as **possible**.
What **business** would it be in?

B. Underline the sight words in sentences 1-4.

1. Could April find work in the same business?

2. Would it be better to work in a different business?

3. How fast is it possible to find a new job?

4. April decided to find out.

C. Write the word that best completes each sentence.

decided   business   possible   fast

1. April read as many want ads as _____ .

2. But _____ was not good for many companies.

3. The jobs in the ads were taken _____ .

4. April _____ not to give up.

D. Read the sentences. Underline the sight words.

"What work can I do?" asked April. "Maybe I can go into a different business." She wanted a job fast, and she decided to find a good one. If she could not find a job as fast as she hoped, then she would keep on trying. April decided that something good would come along. Anything was possible!

Instructor's Notes: Read each set of directions with students. For A, read each sight word aloud and have students repeat it.

5

Unit 1

A. Read the words above. Then read the sentences.

Her home looked **worn**. The **walls** had many **marks**.
April decided to **paint** the walls because she had some time.

B. Underline the sight words in sentences 1–4.

1. April made marks by the ads for jobs she thought she could do.

2. She was worn out from looking for a job.

3. She decided to paint the walls in her home.

4. Soon the walls would shine like new.

C. Write the word that best completes each sentence.

marks   walls   worn   paint

1. April thought her home looked old and _____ .

2. Her home needed a _____ job, and she was the one who could do it.

3. She would fix the holes in the _____ before she began.

4. April decided to ask people not to put _____ on the new paint.

D. Read the sentences. Underline the sight words.

April had a lot of hope as she looked for a job. But some nights she was worn out from looking. When she came back and saw the marks on her walls, she was upset. That's when she decided to paint the walls. "A good paint job is what I need," she said. She didn't know how long the old paint had been on the walls. She did know that new paint would make her home look good and make her feel good.

Instructor's Notes: Read each set of directions with students. For A, read each sight word aloud and have students repeat it. Point out that *mark* and *paint* have more than one meaning in the activities and discuss the meanings.

6

Unit 1

Sight Words

done ● building
color ● under

A. Read the words above. Then read the sentences.

When was the last paint job **done** in this **building**?
What **color** was **under** the worn paint?

B. Underline the sight words in sentences 1–4.

1. April's building was old.

2. Was it possible the color on the walls had once been gray?

3. April looked under the old paint to decide.

4. She asked the owner when painting had last been done.

C. Write the word that best completes each sentence.

under   done   building   color

1. She asked the owner of the _____ if she could paint
   her walls.

2. She invited him to see the paint job after it was _____ .

3. April wanted a light blue, the _____ of the sky.

4. She saw that gray was the color _____ the worn paint.

D. Read the sentences. Underline the sight words.

"Have you done this before?" asked Mr. Lopez, the building owner.

"I painted my home in my other building," said April. "I am fast and neat.
I can do this in under four days."

"Well, you have picked a good color," said Mr. Lopez. "If you do a good
job, I will give you back some money from your rent."

Instructor's Notes: Read each set of directions with students. Encourage students to practice writing sentences from Review Word and Sight Word pages in a notebook or journal.

7

Unit 1

Phonics   -ark and -orn

A. Read the words on the left. Write other -ark words.

l   + ark = _____

p   + ark = _____

sh + ark = _____

sp + ark = _____

-ark

mark

bark

dark

B. Write an -ark word to finish each sentence.

1. April took a walk in the _____ near her building.

2. On her way home, she could hear a dog _____ .

3. April put a _____ by the ads for jobs that she could do.

4. She wanted a light color of paint so her home would not be too

_____ .

C. Read the words on the left. Write other -orn words.

-orn

born

horn

worn

t   + orn = _____

sc + orn = _____

sw + orn = _____

th + orn = _____

D. Write an -orn word to finish each sentence.

1. April had _____ out some ads for jobs.

2. Looking for a new job had _____ her out, but she

had _____ not to give up.

3. April began to feel that she was a _____ painter.

Instructor's Notes: Show students the -ark word pattern in the known sight word mark.
Explain that the r changes the vowel sound. Then read each set of directions with students.
Repeat these steps for the -orn pattern.

Vowels with r

A. A vowel followed by **r** sounds different from the long or short sound of that vowel. Listen to the sound of the vowel with **r** in each word below. Underline the two letters that stand for the first vowel sound in each word.

ar	**ir**	**or**	**er**	**ur**
card	first	born	her	nurse
part	thirst	fork	person	Thursday

B. Make words that have vowels with **r**. Read and write the words.

ar   **ir**

c + ard = _____   sw + irl   = _____

h + ard = _____   tw + irl   = _____

l + ard = _____   wh + irl   = _____

or   **ur**

f + ork = _____   c + urse = _____

st + ork = _____   n + urse = _____

Y + ork = _____   p + urse = _____

C. Write the letters to finish the words below.

1. April is a p __ __ son who works h __ __ d.

2. Her f __ __ st day on the new painting job is Th __ __ sday.

3. The home April will paint is in a building on Y __ __ k Street.

4. It belongs to a n __ __ se she knows.

5. The h __ __ d p __ __ t of the job will be painting over the old dark color.

Instructor's Notes: For A, read the explanation and the sample words. Explain that the vowel sound heard in *r*-controlled vowels is neither long nor short. Read each set of directions with students.

Back to the story...

Remember

What has happened in the story so far?

Predict

Look at the picture. What do you think will happen in the rest of the story?

You Never Know

April took some blue paint home on Monday. She decided if she wasn't working she would get this job done for her family. Her sons Manny and Hector liked the color.

April painted for three days. Mr. Lopez came to look at the walls. He said she had done a fine job. Mr. Sweet from 2B and Mrs. Cruz from 4F came to see her work, too. They liked it so much that they wanted her to paint for them.

April said, "I'm glad you like what I've done. If I can't find a job, I will paint for both of you."

And that is what she did.

Instructor's Notes: Read the questions with students. Help students review and predict. Then have students read the story silently. Use Blackline Master 4: The 5Ws Checklist from the *Instructor's Guide* to help students understand each story in this book. Have students keep their completed checklists in their notebooks or journals.

That Sunday the paper had lots of want ads. April was full of hope again. First she looked under "cleaning." That was the kind of work she had done before for a big company. She marked the jobs she thought would be good. Then she looked at some of the other ads. Was it possible she could get a different kind of job? Did she have to stay in the cleaning business? All at once her eyes saw an ad she liked.

WANTED: Responsible full-time painter. Must be fast, neat, and careful. Need a good eye for color. Apply in person at the Baker Company, 2405 Main St.

As she read the ad, April decided that this was her chance. This was the job for her. First thing on Monday she would go to see about this job. But before she did, she got out her camera and took some color photos of her work. The blue paint looked good. Mr. Sweet in 2B had decided on new tan paint. And Mrs. Cruz in 4F had a light pink color. There will be no more old, worn-looking colors in this building. A painter lives here now.

That Monday April was up at first light. Because she was fast, she was the first one to get to the company where the new job was. She talked to the boss, Mr. Baker.

"This is a small company," Mr. Baker said, "but a friendly one. Still, I have never had a woman painter come in before."

"Give me a chance," said April. "You will see that I'm a good painter. I can do this work well!"

Mr. Baker looked her straight in the eye. "How do I know your skills are good? Have you done jobs that I can see?"

April took out her photos and said, "No problem, I have done a lot of work in this worn-out building. It would be possible for you to see my work and ask the people if they like the jobs I did."

Mr. Baker said he would stop by at the end of the day. That was a long day for April, but a good one. When Mr. Baker came by, she took him to 2B and 4F. He liked what he saw.

"You paint well," he said, "and I've decided to give you a chance. You've got the job."

"Thanks," said April, "you'll be glad you decided on me."

That night April and her sons had a family party.

"It's a good thing you decided to paint," said Hector.

"Right!" said April. "It led to a new career for me. You never know, do you?"

Comprehension

Think About It

1. How did April feel when she got the pink slip?

2. Why did April think she could do the job for Mr. Baker?

3. How did she get Mr. Baker to come to see her work?

4. Sum up what happened in the story.

Write About It

How would you use your time if you lost your job?

Instructor's Notes: Help students read and answer the questions. Write About It can be used as a writing or discussion assignment.

12

Unit 1

Fact and Opinion

A **fact** is something you can prove or see. A fact answers questions such as *who, what, where, when, why, how,* or *how much.*

Example: April painted her home blue.

An **opinion** is how you feel about something. It can tell how you think or what you believe.

Example: Blue is probably the best color for a home.

You will find both facts and opinions in your reading.

Use these tips to help you decide if a sentence states a fact or an opinion.

1. Read the sentence.

2. Decide if it tells about something that can be proved or seen. If so, it is a fact.

3. Does it have word clues such as *I think, I believe, I feel, it seems, probably*? If so, it is an opinion.

Read the sentences. Write _F_ for fact and _O_ for opinion.

1. _____ April went to work for Mr. Baker.

2. _____ "The other painters seem friendly," she thought.

3. _____ "I think I am as good as they are."

4. _____ Her first job is in a big building.

5. _____ The job will probably last three days.

6. _____ April took photos of her work.

7. _____ Painting is the best way to help a building.

8. _____ Women are probably the best painters.

Instructor's Notes: Discuss the tips with students. Then read together the directions for the exercise. Have students write fact and opinion sentences in a notebook or journal.

Subject-Verb Agreement

> **Singular** means one person or thing. **Plural** means more than one person or thing.
>
> With a singular subject, add **-s** to the verb: **paints**
>
> subject   verb
>
> She **paints** the building.
>
> With a plural subject, do not add **-s** to the verb: **paint**
>
> subject   verb
>
> The boys **paint** the building.

A. Draw one line under the subject. Draw two lines under the verb. Read the sentence.

1. April needs a new job.

2. She talks to the owner.

3. The walls need some paint.

4. Mr. Lopez likes April's work.

5. People like the color on the walls.

6. They talk about the colors.

B. Choose the correct verb. Write it in the sentence.

1. Some people _____ the bus to work.
         ride   rides

2. Others _____ to their jobs.
         drive   drives

3. April _____ to work at home.
         hope   hopes

4. She _____ the walls that need paint.
         mark   marks

Instructor's Notes: Discuss the explanation and examples with students. Point out that these rules are about actions that happen in the present.

Some sentences have two or more singular subjects. Two or more singular subjects are called a **compound**. Use the verb without the **-s** because a compound subject is plural.

April and Mr. Lopez **talk** about paint.

The paint and the color **look** good.

April, Mr. Lopez, and Sam **like** the new color.

C. Draw one line under the compound subject. Draw two lines under the verb. Read the sentence.

1. April and Mr. Baker talk about the job.

2. The wall and the door need some paint.

3. The boy and his mom help April.

4. The job and the work make April happy.

5. She and her family get money this way.

6. The job, the money, and the time seem just fine.

D. Choose the correct verb. Write it in the sentence.

1. April and Mr. Baker _____ a plan.
                                       make   makes

2. He and April _____ some help.
                              needs   need

3. Sam, Jan, and Tim _____ April.
                              helps   help

4. The wall and the door _____ better now.
                              look   looks

5. April and her family _____ to paint.
                              like   likes

Instructor's Notes: Discuss the explanation and examples. Have students read the completed sentences aloud.

Reading Help Wanted Ads

A. Read the words. Then read the newspaper help wanted ads.

experienced   references   apartments

B. Read the questions and write the answers.

1. Write the numbers of the ads that ask for painters.

_____

2. a. How are the ads for painters the same?

_____

_____

b. How are they different?

_____

_____

3. Hector wanted a job. It would be his first job. Which of the ads for a painter should he answer?

_____

C. Write about a time you looked for a job.

_____

_____

_____

_____

_____

_____

1	NEEDED: Experienced Route Salesperson. 555-6127
2	NOW ACCEPTING Applications for teachers. The Kids Academy, 555-9789.
3	OWNER OPERATORS for city delivery wanted. Good driving record and good equipment needed. Send resumes to 8305 Woodbury. Do not apply in person.
4	PAINTER/MAKE READY needed at Creek Apartments at 3107 East Oldham. Experienced only. Must have references.
5	PART TIME, FULL TIME opportunity in marketing. Hours flexible. Call Thursday. 555-9000 ext. 3228 for interview.
6	PART TIME groundskeeper needed at apartment complex located North Central. Must maintain grounds and pools. Compensation is apartment only. 555-4651, 555-4706.
7	FULL AND Part Time Cashiers Needed. Apply in person only at 7105 First Street.
8	FULL TIME CASHIER—Monday-Saturday. Must have sewing experience. Call for appointment. New Fabrics, 555-5024.
9	GENERAL PART Time office help. Must have pleasant phone voice. Minimal typing. Interviews on Monday, Tuesday, 8/11, 8/12, 9am–1pm. Call for appointment: 555-7414.
10	GOLD TIME FULL TIME MANAGER APPLY AT NORTH MALL
11	GROUNDSKEEPER/PAINTER— Needed full time. Oaks Apartments. 9112 Mill Road.
12	GYMNASIUM INSTRUCTORS FOR FALL CLASSES 555-7793
13	HELP WANTED at full service station. Mechanical knowledge helpful but not necessary. Come by 1527 Hanford Dr.
14	HOUSEKEEPER NEEDED For Apartment Community. 555-7848.

Instructor's Notes: Read the new words and each set of directions with students. Help them read the ads and answer the questions. For C, point out the icon in the margin and tell students it indicates a place for them to produce their own writing. Use the Unit 1 Review on page 17 to conclude the unit. Then assign *Reading for Today Workbook Five*, Unit 1.

16

Unit 1

A. Write the word that best completes each sentence.

decided	business	possible	fast
marks	full	worn	paint
under	done	building	color

1. April lives in an old _____ .

2. Is it _____ to make it look new?

3. April _____ to do some painting.

4. She ended up in the painting _____ .

B. Write -ark or -orn to make new words. Write each word in the sentence.

1. p + _____ = _____ April's kids play in the _____ near her building.

2. w + _____ = _____ They are _____ out when they come home.

3. th + _____ = _____ One day Hector got a _____ in his hand.

4. sp + _____ = _____ But it did not _____ his mother's attention as much as the time he fell.

C. Add -es to the words. Write the correct word to complete the sentences.

1. bus _____   2. teach _____

3. boss _____   4. box _____

5. April _____ her sons how to paint.

6. They may need to stand on _____ to paint the walls.

7. When April isn't looking, Manny _____ his brother around.

8. They will help after they ride home on the school _____ .

Unit 2 *Buying Goods on Credit*

Discussion

Remember

Look at the picture. What do you think is happening? Have you or a friend ever been in this situation?

Predict

Look at the picture and the story title. What do you think this story is about?

Buying on Time

Ray and Star Pope went shopping for a new bedroom set.

"Look, Ray," said Star, "that one is nice, don't you think? It looks like it's made of pine."

Ray wanted his wife to buy what she liked, but they did not make much money. "I bet that set costs a lot, Star," he said.

"Let's ask how much it is," Star said as she led Ray into the store.

Ray put out his hand and said, "Hold on, Star. Before we buy anything, let's think about it. Don't forget that we have two big bills to pay right now."

Star laughed and gave Ray a hug. "We'll find a way," she said. "These stores let you buy on time, so we could pay bit by bit."

The story continues.

Instructor's Notes: Read the discussion questions with students. Discuss the story title and the situation in the picture. Have students read silently. Have them underline words they don't recognize. Review the underlined words. Have students identify the characters.

Review Words

A. Check the words you know.

☐ **1.** save   ☐ **2.** spend   ☐ **3.** pregnant

☐ **4.** cost   ☐ **5.** table   ☐ **6.** company

☐ **7.** wife   ☐ **8.** bring   ☐ **9.** straight

☐ **10.** baby   ☐ **11.** coupon   ☐ **12.** customer

B. Read and write the sentences. Circle the review words.

1. Ray and his wife can't spend much money.

_____

2. They need some straight talk about cost.

_____

3. Star is pregnant, and she will be glad when she can bring the baby to see her parents.

_____

_____

4. The Popes need to shop with a good company.

_____

C. Read the clues. Write a review word for the answer.

1. something with four legs   _____

2. a person who shops in a store   _____

3. something to save you money   _____

4. to put money away   _____

Instructor's Notes: Read each set of directions with students. For A, have students read the words aloud and then check known words. Have students practice any unknown words in a notebook or journal.

20

Unit 2

Sight Words

afford ● furniture
so ● little

A. Read the words above. Then read the sentence.

The Popes could not **afford** a lot of **furniture** because they had **so little** money and a baby was coming.

B. Underline the sight words in sentences 1–5.

1. The Popes needed furniture, so they went shopping.

2. They could not afford to spend much money.

3. They had saved a little money for furniture.

4. Many furniture sets cost so much that the Popes could not afford them.

5. They hoped to get the furniture and pay a little bit at a time.

C. Write the word that best completes each sentence.

furniture   so   little   afford

1. Star wanted a big bed and a _____ table.

2. "Can we _____ to buy both of them?" she asked.

3. "I hope _____ ," said Ray. "We need them."

4. "Our home will look better with some new _____ ."

D. Read the sentences. Underline the sight words.

Star and Ray wanted to forget about saving money when they saw the furniture they wanted. They liked it so much that they did not want to think about cost. But they could not afford all the furniture at once. Can they buy it a little at a time?

Instructor's Notes: Read each set of directions with students. For A, read each sight word aloud and have students repeat it.

Sight Words

pretty ● credit
check ● name

A. Read the words above. Then read the sentence.

The store does a **pretty** good **credit check** on your **name**.

B. Underline the sight words in sentences 1–5.

1. Star liked the pine set because it was pretty.

2. "Can a customer get credit here?" asked Star.

3. Mr. Silva, who worked in the store, took Ray's and Star's names.

4. Mr. Silva ran a credit check on them.

5. "I checked and your credit is pretty good," he told them.

C. Write the word that best completes each sentence.

name   check   pretty   credit

1. The Popes have good _____ because they pay bills on time.

2. They do _____ well with the pay they get.

3. They try to _____ how much they spend.

4. Customers need to keep a good _____ with stores.

D. Read the sentences. Underline the sight words.

Ray and Star wanted to buy some pretty furniture before the baby came. They checked some ads to see about how much a bedroom set would cost. Ray and Star might have to buy the furniture on credit. They have a good name with credit companies because they pay bills on time.

Instructor's Notes: Read each set of directions with students. For A, read each sight word aloud. Have students repeat. Discuss with students that *pretty* has more than one meaning in the activities.

22

Unit 2

Sight Words

month ● yes
plain ● interest

A. Read the words above. Then read the sentences.

Could the Popes pay a little every **month**?
Yes, but it is **plain** that they would pay **interest**, too.

B. Underline the sight words in sentences 1–3.

1. "Will the bedroom set cost more if we pay month by month?" Star asked.

2. "Yes," said Ray. "It is plain that it will cost more if we buy on time."

3. "That is because you will be paying interest every month," Mr. Silva said.

C. Write the word that best completes each sentence.

month   yes   interest   plain

1. It was _____ to see that Star and Ray wanted the bedroom set.

2. "Will you like paying for it _____ by _____ ?"
Star asked Ray.

3. "_____ ," he said, "that's OK with me."

4. "I want to check on the _____ rates in other stores before we
make up our minds," said Star.

D. Read the sentences. Underline the sight words.

"Do you like this plain bedroom set?" Ray asked.

"Yes," Star said, "but I've been thinking of a pretty one for months."

Could they afford it? Ray and Star were trying to be responsible about
money. They always used coupons when they shopped. They did not want
to get into trouble over heavy interest.

Instructor's Notes: Read each set of directions with students. Discuss with students that
interest has more than one meaning. Encourage students to practice writing sentences from
Review Word and Sight Word pages in a notebook or journal.

23

Unit 2

Phonics   -ain and -ame

A. Read the words on the left. Write other -ain words.

-ain

plain

gain

main

pain

rain

br + ain = _____

ch + ain = _____

st + ain = _____

str + ain = _____

B. Write an -ain word to finish each sentence.

1. Ray liked the pine table, but it had a bad _____ on it.

2. A new bed was the _____ thing they needed.

3. Buying the furniture on credit would not put a _____ on the Popes.

C. Read the words on the left. Write other -ame words.

-ame

name

came

game

same

bl + ame = _____

fr + ame = _____

sh + ame = _____

D. Write an -ame word to finish each sentence.

1. It's a _____ that the table has a stain.

2. A store down the street has the _____ pine furniture set.

3. No one would _____ us if we got the table there.

4. That store has the furniture we _____ to buy.

Instructor's Notes: Show students the *-ain* word pattern in the known sight word *plain*. Explain that the letters *ai* together spell the long *a* sound. Repeat these steps for the *-ame* pattern, explaining that *a* + consonant + *e* spells the long *a* sound. Read each set of directions with students.

Long <u>a</u>

A. The letters **ai**, **ay**, and **a-e** can all stand for the long <u>a</u> sound. Listen for the vowel sound in each word below. Underline the letters that stand for the long <u>a</u> sound.

ai	ay	a-e
plain	day	age
pain	pay	name
paid	play	make

B. Make other long <u>a</u> words. Read and write the words.

-aid

m + aid = _____

r + aid = _____

br + aid = _____

-ay

w + ay = _____

st + ay = _____

gr + ay = _____

-age

p + age = _____

w + age = _____

st + age = _____

-ape

dr + ape = _____

gr + ape = _____

sh + ape = _____

C. Write the vowel letters to make the words.

1. Star likes the sh _ p _ of this pine table.

2. This set will look good with the dr _ p _ s.

3. Ray likes the pl _ _ n black table.

4. Star likes the blue and gr _ _ set better.

5. She thinks about the w _ _ that furniture will look at home.

Instructor's Notes: For A, read the rule and the sample words. Explain that the long *a* sound can be spelled *ai*, *ay*, or *a-e*. Point out an example of each pattern. Read each set of directions with students.

Back to the story...

Remember
What has happened in the story so far?

Predict
Look at the picture. What do you think will happen in the rest of the story?

Buying on Time

Star ran over to the pine bedroom set. She sat on the big bed and looked at the little end tables and the two lights.

Mr. Silva, the man who had checked Ray's and Star's credit, came right over when he saw Star's interest in the set.

"Isn't that a pretty little set?" he said. "I think it's the nicest one in the store, and what a good buy! You can have it for $800."

Instructor's Notes: Read the questions with students. Help students review and predict. Then have students read the story silently.

Mr. Silva walked around the bedroom set talking all the time. There was something fake about him. He said things like credit, no money down, and big savings. But he didn't talk about interest rates. Pretty soon he took out his pad and made out a bill.

"We can get the bedroom set to you today if you put your names here now," he said with a wink at Star.

"Hold on there," said Ray. "My wife and I need time to think this over. We don't buy furniture every day, you know."

"Yes, this is a big event for us, so we want to check it all out," said Star.

Mr. Silva looked down. It was plain to see that these customers were going to take more of his time.

"Tell us about your interest rates," said Ray. "I know that if we buy on time, we'll pay more. If we take 18 months to pay for the furniture, how much interest will we pay?"

Mr. Silva laughed and said, "It's not so much, don't think about it. I know you can afford it, and you'll have the use of the bedroom set for so many more months."

"Yes, Mr. Silva, but how much money in interest are we talking about?" asked Star. "We know what the furniture costs, but what will the interest cost us?"

"I can see that you need to talk to my boss," said Mr. Silva. "When it comes to a good buy, he'll give you the chance of a lifetime."

Star said, "I don't think we want to talk to your boss. I think we want to shop around some more. We want some straight talk about credit and interest rates. You're giving us the run-around."

Ray and Star walked out of the store.

Star and Ray looked some more. They didn't find any furniture that day. It took two months before they once again saw some bedroom furniture they wanted. It was at the Holiday Home Furniture Company. By then they had saved a little more money, and they could afford to put more money down. They could pay a bit more every month, so the bill would be paid sooner.

"I feel much better about this," said Star. "We are buying from a store with a good name, and we will be paying bills we can afford. I think we got a fine bedroom set, too."

Ray said, "Now that we've got the bedroom set, Star, I want to tell you about some more things I've been wanting for our home."

"Let's have it," Star said.

"Sit down," said Ray. "I want a camera, an AM/FM radio, a big TV set, a VCR player, and a newer car."

"You're a kick," said Star, "do you know that? Why don't you run right over to see Mr. Silva? His boss will give you the chance of a lifetime!"

Comprehension

Think About It

1. Why didn't Ray and Star buy the first bedroom set they looked at?

2. How did they feel about Mr. Silva's way of talking?

3. When did Ray and Star find some other bedroom furniture?

4. Sum up what happened in the story.

Write About It

How do you feel about buying on credit? What is good about it? What is not?

Instructor's Notes: Help students read and answer the questions. Write About It can be used as a writing or discussion assignment.

28

Unit 2

Comparing and Contrasting

When you say how two things are alike, you **compare** them.

Example: You can sleep on both a bed and a cot.

When you say how two things are different, you **contrast** them.

Example: A bed is bigger than a cot, but you can put a cot away when you don't need it.

Use these tips to decide if things are compared or contrasted.

1. Read the story.

2. List the facts.

3. Look for clue words such as these that show how two things are alike: *both*, *also*, *similar*, and *like*.

4. Look for clue words such as these that show how two things are different: *however*, *but*, *on the other hand*, *unlike*, and *although*.

Read these sentences. List the facts. Answer the questions.

Both the Holiday Home Furniture Company and the Friendly Furniture Store have credit plans. However, the Holiday Home Furniture Company has better interest rates.

1. _____

2. _____

3. How are the companies alike? What clue word helped you?

_____

4. How are the companies different? What clue word helped you?

_____

Instructor's Notes: Discuss the tips with students. Then read together the directions for the exercise. Have students write comparing and contrasting sentences in a notebook or journal.

> Add the endings **-er** and **-est** to some words to compare things.
>
> small   small**er**   small**est**

A. Read the words. Add -er and -est to make the new words.

	-er	-est
1. old	_____	_____
2. straight	_____	_____
3. neat	_____	_____
4. long	_____	_____
5. tight	_____	_____
6. clean	_____	_____

B. Read the paragraphs. Underline the words that compare things.

"This is a long table, but I want a longer one," said Ray. "My sister has the longest table in the family. We can all sit at that table."

"Our older table will have to do for now. Our money will be tighter when we buy a bedroom set," said Star.

C. Write the word that best completes each sentence.

smaller   longest   cleanest

1. We have been in many stores. Some are clean, but this is the

   _____ store we have seen.

2. This rug is too big. Can we find one that is _____ ?

3. I want a long table. Is this the _____ table you have?

Instructor's Notes: Discuss with students how adding *-er* to a word compares two things and adding *-est* to a word compares more than two. Read each set of directions with students.

30

Unit 2

Use **-er** when you are comparing **two** things.

 This table is **long<u>er</u>** than that one.

Use **-est** when you are comparing **more than two** things.

 This table is the **long<u>est</u>** of the four tables we've seen.

D. Add -er to the word. Write it in the sentence.

1. This bedroom is _____ than ours.

          small

2. The table is _____ than the bedroom set.

       old

3. Is that table _____ than the one we have at home?

       long

E. Add -est to the word. Write the word.

1. Of all three tables, this one is the _____ .

            small

2. I like all four beds, but this one is the _____ .

            long

3. This rug is the _____ of all the ones we have.

       old

F. Write four sentences of your own.

1. Compare two things

_____

_____

2. Compare more than two things

_____

_____

Instructor's Notes: Read the explanation and directions with students. For F, have students read their sentences aloud.

Reading a Payment Schedule

payment   total   insurance

A. Read the words above. Then read the payment schedule.

Payment Schedule

Unpaid Balance $800.00
Property Insurance 48.31
Life Insurance...12.08
Accident & Health Insurance 27.16
Non-Filing Insurance 10.00

Amount Financed 897.55
Finance Charge..188.49
    (@21%)
Total of Payments...1,086.04

APR (Annual Percentage Rate).......................21%

First Payment Due   9/8/01
17 payments at 63.00
1 payment at 15.04

B. Read the questions and write the answers.

1. **a.** What is the total that the Popes will pay over 18 months?

    _____

    b. By taking 18 months to pay for an $800 bedroom set, how much more

    will the Popes pay? _____

2. **a.** When do the Popes need to make the first payment?

    _____

    b. How much is it? _____

    c. How much is the end payment? _____

3. What rate of interest will the Popes pay? _____

Instructor's Notes: Read the new words and each set of directions with students. Help them
read the payment schedule and answer the questions. Use the Unit 2 Review on page 33 to
conclude the unit. Then assign *Reading for Today Workbook Five*, Unit 2.

32

Unit 2

A. Write the word that best completes each sentence.

name	plain	pretty	interest
yes	month	credit	little
so	check	afford	furniture

1. The Popes want to know about _____ rates at this store.

2. They can't _____ to pay all at once for the furniture.

3. Mr. Silva checked their _____ rating.

4. They'll pay a little every _____ for the bedroom set.

B. Write -ain or -ame to make new words. Write each word in the sentence.

1. sh + _____ = _____ It's a _____ that the Popes couldn't buy the bedroom set.

2. bl + _____ = _____ You can't _____ them for wanting it.

3. m + _____ = _____ A new bed was the _____ thing they needed.

4. str + _____ = _____ Buying a bed now would not put a

   _____ on the Popes.

C. Complete each sentence by writing the correct word.

1. That is the _____ table in the store.
   smallest   smaller

2. The Popes have a bed, but they want a _____ one.
   newest   newer

3. This bedroom set is the _____ one in the store.
   finer   finest

4. "This store could be _____ ," said Ray.
   cleanest   cleaner

Unit 3 Sharing Cultures

The Buena Vista Social Club

Discussion

Remember
Look at the picture. What is happening? What kind of music do you like?

Predict
Look at the picture and the story title. What do you think this story is about?

Music for the World

Today people from many different countries are getting together and making music. They mix different ways of playing and singing to make something new. This new music is helping people everywhere understand each other better.

One band that mixes different ways of playing music is the Buena Vista Social Club. The band was started by American guitar player Ry Cooder who loved old-time Cuban music. He went to Cuba to look for the people he had heard on records. They had been famous, but now they were forgotten. One by one, Cooder found them. Some were ninety years old. One worked shining shoes. They could play as well as ever, and they still loved music. They were happy to play together again. Cooder added his slide guitar to the Cuban sound. The band played to full houses all over the world.

Ry Cooder loves discovering different kinds of music. He has played Hawaiian, Indian, African, and Japanese music. He thinks that music brings people together. "We can understand one another if we let music be the key to everything and just respect each other," he says.

The story continues.

Instructor's Notes: Read the photo caption to students and discuss the picture. (Buena: bway-nuh; Vista: vee-stah; Ry: Rie) Read the story title and the discussion questions with students. Have students read the story and underline words they don't recognize. Review the underlined words. Help students read and pronounce *Hawaiian, Indian, African,* and *Japanese.* Use Blackline Master 7: World Map in the *Reading for Today Instructor's Guide* to locate these countries on a world map.

35

Unit 3

Review Words

A. Check the words you know.

☐ **1.** tune   ☐ **2.** players   ☐ **3.** different

☐ **4.** records   ☐ **5.** group   ☐ **6.** fans

☐ **7.** countries   ☐ **8.** listen   ☐ **9.** meet

☐ **10.** people   ☐ **11.** enjoy   ☐ **12.** together

B. Read and write the sentences. Circle the review words.

1. The players come from different countries.

_____

_____

2. They enjoy working together to make a new kind of music.

_____

_____

3. The group has many fans who buy their records.

_____

4. Wherever they play, people come to listen.

_____

C. Match the word with a review word that means almost the same. Write the review word.

_____ **1.** hear

_____ **2.** music

_____ **3.** like

_____ **4.** lands

Instructor's Notes: Read each set of directions to students. For A, have students read the words aloud and then check known words.

Sight Words

musicians ● songs
popular ● died

A. Read the words above. Then read the sentences.

The **musicians'** **songs** were no longer **popular**, but their love of music had not **died**.

B. Underline the sight words in sentences 1-4.

1. They had once been popular musicians.

2. Ry Cooder heard their songs on old records.

3. He thought it would be a shame if their music died.

4. Now their songs are popular in many countries.

C. Write the word that best completes each sentence.

musicians   songs   popular   died

1. The _____ combined their sounds to make a new kind of music.

2. They played old _____ in a new way.

3. Now they are one of the most _____ world music bands.

4. They thought their music had _____, but it came alive again.

D. Read the sentences. Underline the sight words.

Music from other countries has become popular. People in Canada sing songs from Africa, and people in Japan hum tunes from Finland. Musicians bring new ideas to old ways of playing and singing. Many types of music that might have died out have found new life.

Instructor's Notes: Read each set of directions with students. For A, read each sight word aloud and have students repeat it. For D, locate Canada and Finland on the world map, Blackline Master 7 in the *Instructor's Guide.*

37

Unit 3

Sight Words

world • style
instruments • live

A. Read the words above. Then read the sentences.

World music uses all kinds of **instruments**.
It comes in any **style** you can imagine.
Whether it is played **live** or recorded, it is always exciting.

B. Underline the sight words in sentences 1–4.

1. World music begins with the style of a particular place.

2. Players use new instruments to play old music.

3. They combine their music with styles from different parts of the world.

4. When they are ready, they play live for hundreds of people.

C. Write the word that best completes each sentence.

world   style   instruments   live

1. I have some tapes of _____ music.

2. My favorite _____ of music is from Africa.

3. I like to hear the different kinds of _____ .

4. I hope I will get to hear my favorite band play _____ .

D. Read the sentences. Underline the sight words.

   The musicians travel all over the world to play live for their fans.
Everywhere they go they learn about new styles of music. They see strange
instruments. They use some of these new styles and instruments in their
own music.

Instructor's Notes: Read each set of directions with students. For A, read each sight word aloud and have students repeat it.

Sight Words
tradition ● combine
melodies ● rhythms

A. Read the words above. Then read the sentences.

Every group of people has its own musical **tradition**.
World music often **combines** these **traditions** in surprising ways.
The band Mac Umba plays Scottish melodies with Brazilian and
Caribbean **rhythms**.

B. Underline the sight words in sentences 1–4.

1. Her songs have beautiful melodies.

2. Songs with fast rhythms make me want to dance.

3. The guitar combines with other instruments to make a lovely sound.

4. Sad music is a part of their tradition.

C. Write the word that best completes each sentence.

tradition   combine   melodies   rhythms

1. It is hard to keep time to the _____ of that music.

2. It is part of their _____ to clap along with the music.

3. I would like to _____ polka music with Native American chanting.

4. He is always humming different _____ .

D. Read the sentences. Underline the sight words.

When people came to America from Ireland, they brought their musical
tradition with them. In the new country, Irish music combined with other
traditions. You can still hear Irish rhythms and melodies in many American
popular songs.

Instructor's Notes: Read each set of directions with students. Help students read and
pronounce *Scottish*, *Brazilian* and *Caribbean*. Locate Scotland, Brazil, and the Caribbean Sea
on the world map, Blackline Master 7 in the *Instructor's Guide*. Encourage students to practice
writing sentences from Review Word and Sight Word pages in a notebook or journal.

39

Unit 3

A. Read the words on the left. Write other -ie words.

l + ie = _____

t + ie = _____

-ie

die

pie

vie

B. Write an -ie word to finish each sentence.

1. Ry Cooder didn't want to let the old music he loved

_____ out.

2. Some musicians like to _____ new kinds of music with old ones.

3. Do you like to _____ around and listen to CDs?

C. Read the words on the left. Make other -ice words.

r + ice = _____

sl + ice = _____

tw + ice = _____

spl + ice = _____

-ice

price

dice

nice

D. Write an -ice word to finish each sentence.

1. The band played their new song _____ .

2. It's hard for most musicians to make a _____ living from their music.

3. Some fans will pay a big _____ for music on CDs and tapes.

Instructor's Notes: Show students the -ie word pattern in the known sight word die. Read each set of directions with students. Repeat these steps for the -ice pattern. Explain that these words are examples of two different ways to spell the long i sound: both -ie and i + consonant + e stand for long i.

Phonics   Long i

A. **These letters can all stand for the long i sound: ie, i-e, igh, i, and y. Listen for the vowel sound in each word. Underline the letters that stand for the long i sound.**

ie	i-e	igh	i	y
die	rice	right	find	why
tie	five	high	child	try

B. **Make other long i words. Read and write the words.**

i-e

dr + ive = _____

l + ive = _____

thr + ive = _____

igh

br + ight = _____

fr + ight = _____

pl + ight = _____

i

m + ind = _____

w + ind = _____

bl + ind = _____

y

dr + y = _____

sk + y = _____

fl + y = _____

C. **Write the letters to finish the words below.**

1. Some musicians pay a h_____ pr__c__ for their instruments.

2. Their band makes good money, so they don't m__nd the cost.

3. Some popular musicians fl__ all over the world to play their music.

4. They thr__v__ on the fans who buy CDs and tapes.

5. Some musicians have the dr__v__ to make their music into big business.

Back to the story...

Remember

What is <u>world</u> <u>music</u>?

Predict

What happens when people combine styles of music from different parts of the world?

FINLAND

RUSSIA

Music for the World

Värttinä

Have you ever heard of Karelian music? Karelia is a part of Finland and Russia. In the 1980s, a group of Finnish musicians became interested in the Karelian tradition. Karelian music has two different melodies played at the same time. The musicians learned many old Karelian songs. They formed a band and called themselves Värttinä.

The members of Värttinä had new ideas. They wanted to make this music their own. In the tradition of their country, women singers did not sing with instruments, but Värttinä's four women singers got musicians to play along with them. They added pop rhythms and rock and roll energy to the Karelian music. Soon Värttinä had people all over the world singing and dancing to their lively songs.

Today Värttinä plays live all over the world. The group's fans don't know much about Finland or Karelia, but they know the music makes them feel happy.

Värttinä

Instructor's Notes: Read the questions with students. Help students review and predict. Read the photo captions with students. Then have students read the story silently. Point out that foreign words may have accent marks and spellings that are not used in English. Locate Finland and Russia on the world map, Blackline Master 7 in the *Instructor's Guide*.

Papa Wemba

Papa Wemba grew up in a small village in the African country now called Congo. His mother made a living by singing. As a boy Papa Wemba went with her to listen to the music. Then he began to sing with her. Today he still sings in his African language.

Papa Wemba formed a band and began to combine American and Latin pop with African traditions to create new styles of music. When students who had been studying in other countries returned with electric instruments, Papa Wemba and others had everything they needed to invent a new style of dance music called soukous. Soukous first became popular in Congo and then spread all over the world. Papa Wemba says they took one kind of music and made it something different. They made soukous, a new kind of music.

Since those days Papa Wemba has had many bands. Today he is a world music star. Papa Wemba wants to make music for people all over the world. He says that his third record, "Emotion," is music to appeal to Africans, Americans, and Asians.

Papa Wemba

Instructor's Notes: Read the photo caption with students. Have students read the story silently. Point out that *soukous* is pronounced *sue'-koos*.

Angelique Kidjo

Angelique Kidjo has been bringing different worlds together ever since she sang with her brothers and sisters in the Kidjo Brothers Band. She combines many musical traditions, but she never loses sight of her African roots. For one thing, she often keeps rhythm with her mouth. "It goes back to the rhythm where I come from," she says, "and most of the time we play that rhythm without drums. We play it with our mouth, legs, chest, and sometimes, a spoon or coin."

For her record "Fifa," she recorded the sounds of her childhood—drummers, singers, and flute players—and mixed them with musicians from Paris, London, Los Angeles, and San Francisco. The result was a big success. Kidjo does not worry about people who think she should just stick to the African tradition. "My parents taught me you have to respect every style, every culture and every language," she says.

Comprehension

Think About It

1. What is world music?
2. What is Värttinä's home country?
3. What style of music did Papa Wemba help create?
4. Where is Angelique Kidjo's home country of Benin?

Write About It

What's your favorite kind of music?
Who are the stars?
Why do you like their music?

Instructor's Notes: Read the photo captions to students. Help students read and answer the questions. Write About It can be used as a writing or discussion assignment.

44

Unit 3

Comprehension   Sequence

Sequence is about time. It means the order in which things happen.

Use these hints to find the sequence of events in a story:

1. Look for time words like *before*, *when*, *after*, *then*, *always*, *again*, *soon*, *still*, *while*.

2. As you read, try to see the events as if they were part of a movie. Think about the beginning, what comes next, and the end.

A. Reread the story on page 42. Write 1, 2, and 3 to show the correct order of events.

_____   The band called Värttinä was formed.

_____   Two different melodies were used in Karelian music.

_____   Women singers were backed up by instruments when they sang Karelian music.

B. Reread the story on pages 35, 43, and 44. Choose the words that complete each sentence. Circle the letter.

1. The Buena Vista Social Club was started
   a. before Ry Cooder heard old Cuban music.
   b. while the old Cuban musicians were famous.
   c. after Ry Cooder found the old Cuban musicians.
2. Soukous was invented
   a. when Papa Wemba sang with his mother.
   b. before Papa Wemba was a boy.
   c. when Papa Wemba added electric instruments.
3. Angelique Kidjo sang in the Kidjo Brothers Band
   a. when she made the record "Fifa."
   b. before she became famous.
   c. after she became famous.

Instructor's Notes: Discuss the tips with students. Then read the directions together.
Have students write sentences using sequence words in a notebook or journal.

A **friendly letter** is an informal letter, not a business letter. It can be typed or handwritten. A friendly letter might look like the letter below.

[Month, day, year]   June 18, 2000

[Opening]   Dear Sam,

                              Guess what! I have three tickets for Mac Umba
                           on July 8. Can you get off work to come see
                           them? It is their only show in the U.S. this year.
[Main Part]   You can stay with Jan and me. We'd love to see
                           you, and I know you'd hate to miss Mac Umba.

                              Let me know as soon as you can. If you come
                           on the train, I can pick you up on my way home
                           from work.

[Closing]   Your friend,

                                                Ned

A. **Answer these questions about the letter.**

1. When did Ned write the letter? _____

2. Where does the comma go when you write a date? _____

3. Other than the date, what is the first word of the letter? _____

4. What offer does Ned make? _____

5. How does the letter end? _____

B. **Write a letter to someone you know. Use a separate sheet of paper.**

Instructor's Notes: Discuss the parts of a friendly letter. For B, review the parts of a friendly letter with students before they write.

When you address an envelope, include a **mailing address** and a **return address**. A mailing address is the address of the person you're writing to, and the return address is the address of the person sending the letter.

return address

Ned Dean
407 New St.
Compton, NY 12433

mailing address

Sam Best
1219 Center Street
Packway, CT 06008

C. Answer these questions about the envelope.

1. Who is **sending** the letter? _____

   Where does his address go? _____

   What is that address called? _____

2. Who will **receive** the letter? _____

   Where does his address go? _____

   What is that address called? _____

3. Circle the commas on the envelope.

4. Underline the words on the envelope that begin with a capital letter.

5. Circle the ZIP codes on the envelope.

D. Address an envelope for the letter you wrote. Use a real envelope or a separate sheet of paper.

Instructor's Notes: Discuss the parts of an addressed envelope. Point out the ZIP codes and the postal abbreviations for New York and Connecticut. Read each set of directions with students.

Reading a Map

There are four main directions: **north**, **south**, **east**, and **west**. Sometimes they are written **N**, **S**, **E**, and **W**. The **compass rose** shows directions on a map.

A. Look at the compass rose. Read the names of the four directions. Then write the short form for each direction.

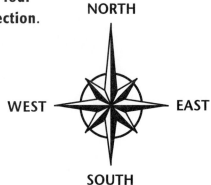

North _____

South _____

East _____

West _____

B. Read the map of North America. Then complete each question with the name of the correct direction.

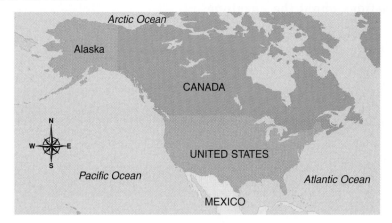

1. Canada is _____ of the United States.

2. The state of Alaska is _____ of Canada.

3. Mexico is _____ of the United States.

4. The Atlantic Ocean is _____ of the United States and Canada.

5. The Pacific Ocean is _____ of Canada, the United States, and Mexico.

6. The Arctic Ocean is _____ of Canada.

Instructor's Notes: Read the information in the box and each set of directions with students. Use the Unit 3 Review on page 49 to conclude the unit. Then assign *Reading for Today Workbook Five*, Unit 3. Preteach the words *Tejano* (teh-há-no) and *Texas* before students read the workbook story for this unit.

A. Write the word that best completes each sentence.

died	popular	live	style
songs	world	musicians	tradition
combine	melodies	instrument	rhythms

1. The _____ come from many countries.

2. They play music all over the _____ .

3. They seem to get more _____ every year.

4. I really like the _____ of that music.

B. Write -ie or -ice to make new words. Write the word that fits best in each sentence.

1. tw + _____ = _____ I saw that band _____ .

2. d + _____ = _____ Their music will not _____ .

3. pr + _____ = _____ What is the _____ for a ticket?

4. l + _____ = _____ I won't _____ about the price.

C. Write a letter to a friend telling about a band you like.

_____

_____

_____

_____

_____

_____

_____

_____

_____

Unit 4   Teaching Children About Safety

Discussion

Remember

Look at the picture. What do you think is happening? Have you ever felt like this?

Predict

Look at the picture and the story title. What do you think this story is about?

A Safe Home

There go my two kids. The little one is so cute, and my older one is getting so big. They're going out to play in the park. The big child has his bat. He's nuts about baseball. Lan is tagging after him like she always does. Ming will look out for her. He's pretty responsible with his little sister.

I check on them from time to time. I go out and yell to them every now and then. They mind me—they don't give me a bad time like some people's kids do. People tell me, "Kim, your kids are so good."

Sometimes I don't like the kids I see around here. They don't live here, but they come around all the time. You can tell they're up to no good. They're looking for trouble, I always say. I tell Ming and Lan to come in right away if they think trouble is coming.

If I had my way, we wouldn't live here. We'd have a nicer home where my kids could play without problems. But, that's not how things are, so we try to make the best of it.

The story continues.

Instructor's Notes: Read the discussion questions with students. Discuss the story title and the situation in the picture. Read the discussion questions with students. Discuss the story title and the situation in the picture. Have students read silently. Have them underline words they don't recognize. Review the underlined words. Have students identify the characters.

51

Unit 4

Review Words

A. Check the words you know.

☐ **1.** kids   ☐ **2.** never   ☐ **3.** could

☐ **4.** or   ☐ **5.** always   ☐ **6.** every

☐ **7.** late   ☐ **8.** mean   ☐ **9.** party

☐ **10.** club   ☐ **11.** once   ☐ **12.** around

B. Read and write the sentences. Circle the review words.

1. Some mean kids live around here.

_____

2. I never come home late from a party or movie.

_____

3. Every person who lives here could help make this a safer place.

_____

_____

C. Read the clues. Write a review word for the answer.

1. a group you might be invited to join _____

2. all the time _____

3. one time _____

4. a fun event _____

5. not on time _____

6. children _____

7. not nice _____

Instructor's Notes: Read each set of directions with students. For A, have students read the words and then check known words. Have students practice any unknown words in a notebook or journal.

Sight Words
show ● very
guard ● protect

A. Read the words above. Then read the sentence.

Can you **show** us how a **very** good **guard** could **protect** our building?

B. Underline the sight words in sentences 1–4.

1. It isn't very safe for kids to play here.

2. A guard could help to protect the kids.

3. We asked the owners of the building to help us protect our homes.

4. They were very nice but didn't show much interest in our problems.

C. Write the word that best completes each sentence.

show   guards   protect   very

1. We need more _____ in this building.

2. No one can come home _____ late.

3. We must _____ the owners that we need help.

4. We can all work together to _____ the kids.

D. Read the sentences. Underline the sight words.

Zack, a small child who lives in 10A, had a very bad time this month. Some mean kids came into the building. They asked Zack to show them his video games. He got very upset and ran away from them. His family is new in the building, so he didn't know who could protect him.

Zack is OK now, but his mother is still very upset. She wants to get some guards in the building to help protect Zack and all the other little kids.

Instructor's Notes: Read each set of directions with students. For A, read each sight word aloud and have students repeat it.

53

Unit 4

A. Read the words above. Then read the sentence.

We want the guards to **watch any strangers** on the **grounds**.

B. Underline the sight words in sentences 1–5.

1. We can't let any strangers come into the building.

2. Some of them make trouble on the grounds.

3. I tell my kids not to talk to any strangers.

4. We need a guard to watch the grounds.

5. A guard won't let strangers onto the grounds.

C. Write the word that best completes each sentence.

　　any　　grounds　　watch　　strangers

1. At first, the people who live together in a building are _____ .

2. They need to _____ who tries to come in.

3. We can all use _____ help we can get.

4. We must guard the _____ .

D. Read the sentences. Underline the sight words.

　　Some strangers are very friendly, but at our building we can't take any chances. I was coming home late one night after a party. I wasn't watching when some strangers came into the building grounds after me. I didn't know any of them and didn't know if they lived here. I found my key and went in. Then they came after me and hit me. I yelled for help. I was lucky that Mr. Price, the guard, was around. The men were arrested. Later, I told Mr. Price how glad I am that he is here on the grounds.

Instructor's Notes: Read each set of directions with students. For A, read each sight word aloud. Have students repeat.

54

Unit 4

Sight Words

kind • town
alone • worry

A. Read the words above. Then read the sentence.

Ming is the **kind** of kid who likes going around **town alone**, and I **worry** about him.

B. Underline the sight words in sentences 1–5.

1. This kind of building is like a small town.

2. Still, I worry when my kids go out alone.

3. I worry that I cannot watch them all the time.

4. Not all strangers will be kind to children.

5. Ming must learn to get around town alone.

C. Write the word that best completes each sentence.

town   worry   alone   kind

1. Ming and Lan are the _____ of kids who don't stay home much.

2. Ming tells me not to _____ when he is out late at night.

3. Now that he's older, he thinks he can get around town _____ .

4. I tell him that this is not always a friendly _____ .

D. Read the sentences. Underline the sight words.

I cannot keep my job and still be with my kids all the time. If we lived in a small town or in the country, maybe I could do it. But here, in this building in a big city, it's not safe for the kids to be alone. I worry because I've had problems and want to keep my kids from having the same kind of trouble.

Instructor's Notes: Read each set of directions with students. For A, read each sight word aloud. Have students repeat. Have students practice writing sentences from Review Word and Sight Word pages in a notebook or journal.

Phonics

-ound and -own

A. Read the words on the left. Write other -ound words.

-ound

grounds

around

found

h + ound = _____

m + ound = _____

s + ound = _____

r + ounds = _____

B. Write an -ound word to finish each sentence.

1. We need to put a fence _____ the grounds.

2. I feel safe at night when a guard is making his _____ .

3. I called the guard when there was a strange _____ in the back room.

C. Read the words on the left. Write other -own words.

-own

town

crown

down

br + own = _____

dr + own = _____

fr + own = _____

cl + own = _____

D. Write an -own word to finish each sentence.

1. Our guard looks mean because of his _____ , but he is a good guard.

2. We can tell who the guards are because they have

    _____ uniforms.

3. After the owners do what we've asked, this building will be

    one of the best ones in our _____ .

Instructor's Notes: Show students the *-ound* word pattern in the known sight word *grounds*.
Then read each set of directions with students. Repeat these steps for the *-own* pattern. Explain
that *-ou* and *-ow* stand for the same vowel sound in these words.

Phonics -ou and -ow

A. The letters ou and ow can stand for the same sound. Listen for the vowel sound in each word. Underline the letters that stand for the vowel sound.

1. found   mound
   pound   out

2. town   brown
   clown   how

B. Make other words with ou and ow.

ou	ow
sh + out = _____	v + ow = _____
spr + out = _____	br + ow = _____

C. The letters ou can stand for more than one sound. Listen for the vowel sound in each word. Underline the letters that stand for the vowel sound.

ou in found

shout   pound
mound   wound

ou in you

group   coupon
soup

D. The letters ow can stand for more than one sound. Listen for the vowel sound in each word. Underline the letters that stand for the vowel sound.

ow in down

how   brown
frown   gown

ow in know

show   own
grow   known

E. Write the vowel letters to make words below.

1. I don't want my kids to gr____ ____ up in this building.

2. I've made a v____ ____ to get them out of here.

3. Some children are on their ____ ____ n much of the time.

Instructor's Notes: For A, C, and D, read the words aloud. Have students repeat. Explain that *ou* and *ow* can stand for more than one sound. Have students tell which sounds are alike and which are different. Read each set of directions with students.

Back to the story...

Remember
What has happened in the story
so far?

Predict
Look at the picture. What do you
think will happen in the rest of
the story?

A Safe Home

Lan came home from school with some good tips today. She learned how to keep our home and family safe. She said all the kids went to a big meeting at school and talked about how to stay safe.

Some parents came to the meeting and told the kids their story. In April, their little son went out to play, and they couldn't find him for two days. The parents were sick with worry. They were so glad when they found their son. They wanted to protect other children, so they told their story to the kids at Lan's school. Then a social worker gave every child a list of tips.

I've made up some tips of my own for parents. I'm going to take my list to a meeting here in the building. I hope we can work out better ways to keep our homes and children safe.

Instructor's Notes: Read the questions with students. Help students review and predict. Then have students read the story silently.

These are the tips I will talk about:

1. Tell your children not to talk to strangers in cars, in parks, or on the streets.

2. Know where your children are at all times. Teach them not to go out without telling you first. When they do go out, find out where they'll be.

3. Know who your children's friends are and where they live.

4. Don't let little children stay at home alone. Get someone to watch them.

5. Tell children of all ages not to let anyone in if you are not home.

6. Teach little children to remember their names and where they live.

•••

The meeting at our building went very well. Most of the parents have been as worried as I have been. People who live alone are interested in helping, too. They think that if the building is safe for kids, it will be safe for everyone.

The building owners listened to us at this meeting. I think they could see by our plain talk that we will not be stopped. They can't afford to look away when we are working so hard. The day after the meeting, Ming and I went around to see every renter. We asked people to tell us how they would make the building safer.

A few days later, a group of renters met with the owners again and told them what we wanted. The owners said they would do some things to help us.

They're going to put more guards on the building grounds. The guards will stop all strangers and find out what they are doing or who they want to see. The guards will look out for the kids who live in the building, too, and see that they don't get into trouble.

At night the gates around the grounds will be locked at nine. Only people who live here will have keys. A guard will stay by the gate to check out the people who come and go.

City cops will work with our guards. They'll back up our guards by giving tickets, protecting us from troublemakers, and showing up when they are needed.

A list of tips for keeping children safe will be sent to all renters. Parents will be responsible for teaching their children to play it safe and to keep these tips in mind at all times.

We think that most people here in the building will be responsible and try to help. Parents, disabled people, older people, and children all have a lot to lose if we don't help each other.

Comprehension

Think About It

1. Why was Kim worried?
2. How did Kim and the other parents get the building owners to listen to them?
3. What was the building like after the meetings on safety?
4. Sum up what happened in the story.

Write About It

What would you have done in this same situation?

Instructor's Notes: Help students read and answer the questions. Write About It can be used as a writing or discussion assignment.

60

Unit 4

Comprehension

Inference

An **inference** is a judgment that you make when you put together new facts with what you know.

Example: You know that there has been trouble in apartment 6G. When you see two cops walk into the building, you **infer** that there is more trouble in 6G.

Use these tips to make an inference.

1. Read the story.

2. List the facts.

3. Add the story facts to what you know.

4. Make an inference. Then think: Do the facts support my thinking?

A. Read this paragraph.

People from an apartment building in a different part of the city came to see Kim. They asked about the way things were being done at Kim's building. They wanted to make their building safe, too.

B. List the facts.

1. _____

2. _____

3. _____

C. Add the story facts to what you have just read. Then choose the best inference. Underline it.

1. People in other parts of the city lived in safety.

2. Kim's work had helped to make her building safer.

3. People came to tell Kim what to do.

Instructor's Notes: Discuss the tips with students. Then read together the directions for the exercises.

> Some action words end in **y**. Before adding an ending to these
> words, change the **y** to **i**.
>
> > try   tries   tried

A. Write the word in each pair with the -ies or -ied ending.

1. cry, cries   _____

2. baby, babies   _____

3. worried, worry   _____

4. carried, carry   _____

5. pries, pry   _____

B. Draw a line to match each word to another form of the word.

1. party   fried

2. baby   carries

3. fry   partied

4. carry   tried

5. try   babies

C. Read the paragraph. Underline the words that end in -ies and -ied.

Lan cries when I tell her not to go out alone. Ming says that I have
babied her too much. Time flies and she is getting older, but I still worry.
Once, she couldn't find her way home. How I worried then! Now Lan
belongs to a club and plays with kids her own age.

Instructor's Notes: Discuss with students changing y to i before adding *-es* or *-ed* when
the y is preceded by a consonant. Read each set of directions with students.

D. Write the word that best completes each sentence.

cried   tries   carried   worries

1. Lan _____ not to talk to strangers.

2. Once, a woman in our building _____ for days because some people took all her furniture.

3. They _____ it off and no one stopped them.

4. Now she _____ that they will come back.

E. To write the new words, drop the letter **y**. Then add **-ies** or **-ied**.

	-ies	-ied
cry	_____	_____
spy	_____	_____
baby	_____	_____
worry	_____	_____
carry	_____	_____

F. What makes a home safe to you? Write three sentences and use a word with an **-ies** or **-ied** ending in each sentence.

_____

_____

_____

_____

_____

_____

Instructor's Notes: Read each set of directions with students. For F, discuss with students the sentences and words with *-ies* or *-ied* endings that they will use.

63

Unit 4

Telephone Safety

telephone   number   emergency   address

A. Read the words above. Then read the tips in the booklet that children should know when they answer the telephone.

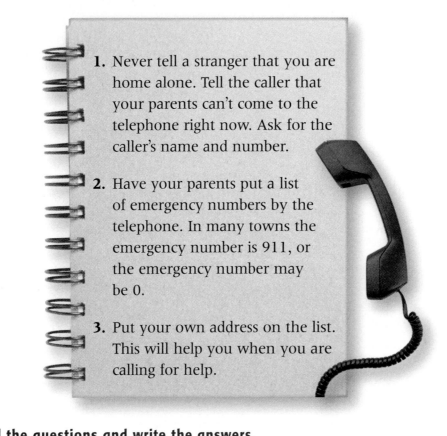

1. Never tell a stranger that you are home alone. Tell the caller that your parents can't come to the telephone right now. Ask for the caller's name and number.

2. Have your parents put a list of emergency numbers by the telephone. In many towns the emergency number is 911, or the emergency number may be 0.

3. Put your own address on the list. This will help you when you are calling for help.

B. Read the questions and write the answers.

1. Your child is home alone. A stranger calls and asks to talk with you. Write what your child should say.

   _____

   _____

2. Why is it good to have your address and telephone number by the phone for a child to use in an emergency?

   _____

   _____

Instructor's Notes: Read the new words and each set of directions with students. Help them read the booklet and answer the questions. Use the Unit 4 Review on page 65 to conclude the unit. Then assign *Reading for Today Workbook Five*, Unit 4.

Unit 4 Review

A. Write the word that best completes each sentence.

show	worry	kind	stranger
guard	alone	town	grounds
very	watch	any	protect

1. Most parents _____ when their kids are out late.

2. Kim tells Lan and Ming not to go out _____ at night.

3. She says the _____ are not very safe after dark.

4. We need a _____ to watch the people who come and go.

B. Write -ound or -own to make new words. Write each word in a sentence.

1. t + _____ = _____ The building isn't the safest spot in

   _____ .

2. ar + _____ = _____ People _____ here worry about their families.

3. f + _____ = _____ People in other buildings have

   _____ that guards can protect them.

4. d + _____ = _____ We'll go _____ to the meeting room to see the owners.

C. Add -es or -ed to the word. Write the word.

1. **(carry)** The guard at the building _____ a gun.

2. **(worry)** Kim _____ if Ming isn't home by sundown.

3. **(cry)** When Kim made Lan stay home from a party, she _____ .

4. **(try)** Kim met with the owners and _____ to tell them about problems in the building.

Discussion

Remember
Look at the picture. How do you think this woman is feeling? Have you ever felt like this?

Predict
Look at the picture and story title. What do you think this story is about?

Some Really Good "Failures"

Carla walked home slowly. It hadn't been a very good day. Her son Rocky had given her trouble before he went to school. Ninth grade wasn't going well for him, and he was always looking for ways to stay home. He wouldn't listen to her when she tried to make him feel better about things.

Carla knew Rocky was upset, and now she felt the same way. Her boss at work had yelled at her today and said she made too many mistakes. Carla was worried. She couldn't let Rocky's problems bring them both down. He needed her and she would find a way to help him.

"I'm not going to let all this get to me," Carla decided. "Other people overcome things, and Rocky can, too!"

The story continues.

Instructor's Notes: Read the discussion questions with students. Discuss the story title and the body language of the woman in the picture. Ask students why they think *failure* is in quotation marks. Have students read the story silently. Have them underline words they don't recognize. Review the underlined words.

67

Unit 5

Review Words

A. Check the words you know.

☐ 1. school ☐ 2. ninth ☐ 3. because

☐ 4. wrong ☐ 5. interest ☐ 6. always

☐ 7. slowly ☐ 8. listen ☐ 9. knew

☐ 10. problems ☐ 11. desk ☐ 12. cope

B. Read and write the sentences. Circle the review words.

1. Rocky was down because he was not doing well in school.

_____

_____

2. Carla worried that he had lost interest in ninth grade.

_____

_____

3. Carla had her own problems to cope with at work.

_____

C. Read the clues. Write a review word for the answer.

1. opposite of <u>never</u>   _____

2. furniture to work at   _____

3. not right   _____

4. past form of <u>know</u>   _____

5. not fast   _____

6. hear   _____

Instructor's Notes: Read each set of directions with students. For A, have students read the words and then check known words. Have students practice any unknown words in a notebook or journal.

Sight Words

joy • failure
those • programs

A. Read the words in above. Then read the sentences.

Rocky's failure in those programs took all the joy out of school for him.

B. Underline the sight words in sentences 1–4.

1. Many people have seemed to be failures in school work.

2. Lots of those people go on to do very well.

3. It is hard to feel joy if you feel like a failure.

4. Most schools have programs for those who need help.

C. Write the word that best completes each sentence.

those   program   joy   failure

1. Rocky needed the right kind of reading _____ .

2. Carla wanted him to find _____ in reading.

3. Carla knew that a feeling of _____ could drive Rocky from school.

4. She hoped Rocky would work on _____ reading skills.

D. Read the sentences. Underline the sight words.

One night Carla and Rocky watched a program together on TV. It was about people who seemed to be failures but went on to do very well. Some of those people were popular musicians. Others had top careers as writers, senators, doctors, and business leaders. "Anything is possible," thought Carla as she watched the program. She could tell from the joy in his eyes that Rocky had this feeling, too.

Instructor's Notes: Read each set of directions with students. For A, read each sight word aloud and have students repeat it. Explain to students that many people with reading problems have a disorder called dyslexia. Experts think dyslexia is inherited; it has nothing to do with laziness or intelligence.

just ● spoil ● really
success ● brace

A. Read the words above. Then read the sentences.

Even something like needing a leg **brace** won't **spoil** your chances.
Just work **really** hard, and you'll find **success**.

B. Underline the sight words in sentences 1–5.

1. No one really wants to be a failure.

2. Some people just take longer to find their way.

3. Success means different things to different people.

4. Some people who wear leg braces learn to be top runners.

5. A bad outlook can really spoil your chances of success.

C. Write the word that best completes each sentence.

just   really   spoil   success   brace

1. Carla hoped that Rocky would have some _____ in school.

2. She didn't want his reading problems to _____ things for him.

3. Reading was _____ hard for him.

4. It _____ didn't seem right that he had so much trouble.

5. Rocky didn't need any kind of _____ .

D. Read the sentences. Underline the sight words.

Carla and Rocky were really interested to learn about all the successful people who had had problems. These people didn't let their problems spoil things for them. They just kept trying. One man became a big success as a stockbroker. He made a lot of money. Reading was just harder for him than for some people. Other people who wore leg braces went on to become top sports stars.

Instructor's Notes: Read each set of directions with students. For A, read each sight word aloud. Have students repeat. Explain that people with dyslexia have a problem connecting symbols (letters) with sounds.

Sight Words

impulse ● answer
order ● famous

A. Read the words on the left. Then read the sentences.

On an **impulse**, Carla decided to **answer** a mail **order** ad.
She sent for a video about **famous** people who did not do well at first.

B. Underline the sight words in sentences 1–4.

1. Carla does not buy many things on impulse.

2. She wanted to order this video for Rocky.

3. The video might have some answers for him.

4. It would show him that many famous people had problems before they found success.

C. Write the word that best completes each sentence.

order   answer   impulse   famous

1. Carla doesn't know the _____ to Rocky's problems.

2. She doesn't want to _____ him to go to school.

3. Her _____ to help him with his problems is a good one.

4. Many _____ people had trouble in school.

D. Read the sentences. Underline the sight words.

On an impulse Carla checked with the video company to see how soon her order would be sent. She got an answer right away. Her order for the "Famous Failures" video was in the mail. Carla told Rocky about her impulse order. His answer gave her hope.

"The TV show about famous people with problems was interesting," he said. "So maybe the video will be, too. It was a good impulse, Mom. I'm glad you ordered that video."

Instructor's Notes: Read each set of directions with students. For A, read each sight word aloud and have students repeat it. Discuss with students that *answer* and *order* can be used in more than one way. Have students continue journal writing.

Phonics -oil and -oy

A. Read the words on the left. Write other -oil words.

-oil

spoil

boil

soil

c + oil = _____

f + oil = _____

t + oil = _____

br + oil = _____

B. Write an -oil word to finish each sentence.

1. School was hard for Rocky, who had to _____ to overcome his problems.

2. Carla didn't want school problems to _____ Rocky's success in life.

3. When she came home from work, Carla put the water on to

   _____ .

C. Read the words on the left. Write other -oy words.

-oy

Roy

boy

coy

j + oy = _____

s + oy = _____

t + oy = _____

D. Write an -oy word to finish each sentence.

1. Helping Rocky with his reading problems gives Carla a lot of

   _____ .

2. Rocky is no longer a little _____ , so they must find an answer to his problems now!

3. Carla and Rocky cannot _____ with failure. They must really work for success.

Instructor's Notes: Show students the *-oi* word pattern in the known sight word *spoil*. Then read each set of directions with students. Repeat these steps for the *-oy* pattern. Explain that the *oi* and *oy* stand for the same sound in these words. Point out that *y* acts as a vowel in the patterns *-oy*, *-ay*, and *-ey*.

A. The letters oi can be found at the beginning or in the middle of a word. Read each word and underline oi.

oil	spoil	choice
oily	join	noise
ointment	point	hoist
coin	poison	

B. The letters oy can be found in the beginning, in the middle, or at the end of a word. Read each word and underline oy.

oyster	joy	boycott
boy	annoy	employ
loyal	toy	disloyal
voyage	ahoy	joyful

C. Write oi or oy to make words.

1. Rocky knows that it will ann_____ Carla if he just gives up on his school work.

2. He tries hard, but sometimes he says, "What's the

   p_____nt?"

3. Rocky doesn't want his learning problems to sp_____l his chances of success in life.

4. He wants to be someone a boss would like to empl_____ .

5. Carla says that Rocky must make good ch_____ces and really work hard for success.

Instructor's Notes: Read each word aloud and have students repeat it. Read each set of directions with students.

73

Unit 5

Back to the story...

Remember
What has happened in the story
so far?

Predict
What do you think will happen in
the rest of the story? Why?

Some Really Good "Failures"

Carla ordered a video for Rocky. It turned out to be a big hit.
Rocky watched it as soon as it came. "A lot of people have to
really work for their success," Carla said. She tried to talk to
Rocky about the lives of those people, but he just nodded and
didn't answer. So Carla let it drop. She didn't want to spoil his
enjoyment of the video.

Then one night when Carla came home from work, she saw
that Rocky had been watching the video again. On an impulse,
she asked him about it. "What part do you like best?" she asked.

Instructor's Notes: Read the questions with students. Help students review and predict.
Then have students read the story silently.

74

Unit 5

"There's this woman named Wilma Rudolph," he answered. "She was a really famous track star in the 1960s. She was one of 22 children. When she was just four, she got really, really sick."

"Go on," Carla said.

Rocky tapped his leg. "She got over that illness, but she lost the use of her left leg. She had to use braces to walk."

"So how did Wilma Rudolph become a track star?"

"She just worked at it. First she learned how to walk again. Her brothers and sisters helped her. Then, one day she took off those braces and walked. Her mother and the doctor were shocked!"

"Walking was Rudolph's first success then," said Carla.

"Right, then she went on to become a really fast runner. She won three golds in the Olympics in 1960," said Rocky. "She led the way for both blacks and women in this sport," Rocky went on. "And when she quit running, she set up track programs so that other boys and girls could have a chance at success."

Wilma Rudolph

"I really like that story," said Carla. She was careful not to say anything more to Rocky about working for success. A week or two went by. Then one Sunday night Rocky played the video again. This time Carla watched, too. Rocky stopped the video at a part about a doctor.

"He's not famous like Wilma Rudolph," he said, "but he's still a real success story. Dr. Ben Carson was one of those kids who felt like a failure. He didn't know his father when he was a boy. He didn't think he was smart, and he didn't do well in school," Rocky said. "He became a successful doctor. He is famous for his work with brain problems in children."

"That's really something," said Carla. She was also thinking, "You are a little like this man, Rocky. Do you see that?"

Dr. Benjamin Solomon Carson

After that Carla let Rocky be. She could tell he was thinking about failure and how it can lead to success.

Instructor's Notes: If necessary, help students read the word *Olympics*. Ask students if they have ever watched the Olympics on TV.

Two weeks later, Carla got a card from Rocky's teacher. Could she come in to school? Carla was worried. What did the teacher want? What was going on with Rocky? On Friday, she took time off from work and went to the meeting.

"You know, I've been worried about Rocky all year," the teacher said. "He has problems with reading that really slow him down. I know it's hard for him. He feels bad so much of the time. But this week he was a real success. He gave a report on people who overcame problems. It was just the best! The other kids really listened. I think they all learned something of value—about the people in the report and about people right here in this school."

Carla was overjoyed. It looked like Rocky was going to get over his problems. It would be hard, but she vowed to stand by him every step of the way and see that he got all the help he needed. At last Rocky was going for success!

Comprehension

Think About It

1. Why wasn't Rocky doing well in school?
2. How did Carla make Rocky see that he could overcome his problem?
3. How did Rocky feel after he saw the video?
4. Sum up what happened in the story.

Write About It

What problem do you have that might be keeping you from success? Tell about it and what you might do to overcome it.

Instructor's Notes: Help students read and answer the questions. Write About It can be used as a writing or discussion assignment.

76

Unit 5

Making Judgments

When you make a **judgment**, you put a value on something. You decide about something. You form an opinion based on some reasons. For example, you might think: What will be the outcome if I try to do something that's really hard for me? I might have success, but then again, I might meet with failure.

Use these tips to make judgments about your reading.

1. Read the story.

2. Decide what you think. Ask things like: What are my reasons? What will the results be? How could I defend this? What values am I using here?

A. Read this paragraph.

Carla was having trouble learning a new part of her job. This assignment was really hard for her, yet she had learned new things before. Carla didn't want her boss to know about her problem. He might think she was a failure.

B. Use facts from the story and the paragraph above to answer the questions.

1. What things should Carla think about as she decides what to do?

_____

_____

_____

2. What would you tell Carla to do? Why?

_____

_____

_____

Instructor's Notes: Discuss the tips with students. Then read together the directions for the activities.

77

Unit 5

> To make most nouns plural, add an **s.**
>   Example: **brother** (one)   **brothers** (more than one)
> To make a noun show ownership, add **'s**. This makes a singular possessive noun.
>   Example: **brother**   one **brother's** room
> To make a plural noun show ownership, just add an apostrophe (').
> This makes a plural possessive noun.
>   Example: My two **brothers'** cars will not run.

A. Decide if the possessive noun is singular or plural. Write singular or plural.

1. reader's book _____

2. doctors' instruments _____

3. mother's worries _____

4. teachers' school _____

B. Read the paragraph. Underline the possessive nouns.

Rocky's interest in reading problems led him to set up a web site. He likes to read the visitors' e-mails. Many women's letters ask about Rocky's mother. Some of the letters tell about a kid's reading success or a school's reading program. Other writers' e-mails ask about the video's stories.

C. Change each noun to make it show ownership. Write the plural possessive noun.

1. learners _____

2. parents _____

3. runners _____

4. helpers _____

5. sisters _____

Instructor's Notes: Discuss with students how possessives are formed for singular and plural nouns. Read each set of directions with students.

D. Decide if the noun is singular or plural. Then add 's or ' to make it possessive.

1. Carla _____ son

2. strangers   many _____ letters

3. radio   the _____ program

4. legs   both _____ braces

5. boys   three _____ homework

E. Underline the words in each sentence that should be possessive. Then write the sentence correctly.

1. This books words are hard, but those books words are not.

   _____

2. Too many failures can add to a kids troubles.

   _____

3. The girls successes came from her fathers help.

   _____

F. Write three sentences of your own.

1. Write a sentence with a plural noun.

   _____

2. Write a sentence with a plural possessive noun.

   _____

3. Write a sentence with a singular possessive noun.

   _____

Instructor's Notes: Read each set of directions with students. For F, discuss the correct forms of the nouns that students will use in their sentences.

Reading a Chart

scientist   important   medical

A. Read the words. Then read the chart.

Successful "Failures"		
Name	**Problem**	**Success**
Pablo Picasso	He did so badly in school, his father took him out at age 10.	He became one of the most famous painters of his time.
Elizabeth Blackwell	She wanted to be a doctor in a time when there were no women doctors, but 29 medical schools turned her down.	She became the first woman doctor in the United States.
Winston Churchill	He failed sixth grade.	He became one of England's most important leaders.
Albert Einstein	He didn't speak until he was four.	He became one of the world's most famous scientists.

B. Read the questions and write the answers.

1. What problem did Elizabeth Blackwell have to overcome?

   _____

2. Who failed sixth grade?

   _____

3. What was Albert Einstein's success?

   _____

4. Who was Pablo Picasso?

   _____

5. Which of these people do you most admire? Why?

   _____

   _____

Instructor's Notes: Read the new words and each set of directions with students. Help them read the chart and answer the questions. Use the Unit 5 Review on page 81 to conclude the unit. Then assign *Reading for Today Workbook Five*, Unit 5. Preteach the word *India* before students read the workbook story.

A. Write the word that best completes each sentence.

programs	just	famous	those
spoil	failure	really	hard
impulse	order	answer	success

1. Carla wanted to help Rocky have _____ .

2. She knew he sometimes felt like a _____ .

3. She was glad there were school _____ to help.

4. Rocky needed to work _____ .

B. Write -oil or -oy to make new words. Write each word in a sentence.

1. j + _____ = _____ Reading didn't give Rocky any

   _____ .

2. sp + _____ = _____ Carla didn't want failure to

   _____ his chances.

3. s + _____ = _____ He helped her order bags of

   _____ to put on the grass.

4. t + _____ = _____ They found an old _____
   under a tree.

C. Add 's or s' to the word at the left. Write the correct word to complete the sentence.

1. **(Rocky)** The name of _____ video was "Famous Failures."

2. **(program)** Two school _____ success was real.

3. **(boy)** All _____ problems are not the same.

4. **(mother)** Most _____ impulses are good.

Unit 6 Following Immigration Procedures

Discussion

Remember
Look at the journal. Have you ever kept a journal like this?

Predict
Look at the title. What do you think this journal tells about?

A Home Away From Home

June 14

It's hard to remember that I've only been here about a year. In some ways I feel that it's been longer. I feel so much at home here — the Prices are like my family. I like looking after their kids, Shelly and Ike, and helping to run their home. We all get along well together. The Prices are always saying, "What would we do without you, Pam?" And Mrs. Price's friend who lives down the street says, "I want someone just like you to help me when I have children."

But the letter I got today from my sister Rose made me feel homesick. She has always been my best friend as well as my sister, and I'm lonely when I think of her. It's hard to make friends in a new country. I don't meet many people because I work here in the Price's home. Also, I'm shy about talking to strangers when I go out on my day off.

Sometimes I wish I could go home to see Rose, but I can't afford it. Anyway, I can't take that much time off because the Prices need me. How can they go to <u>their</u> jobs without someone to help out at home? I'll have to find another way... maybe Rose could come to see me.

The story continues.

Instructor's Notes: Read the discussion questions with students. Help students review and predict. Then have the students read silently. Have them underline words they don't recognize. Review the underlined words. Have students tell what the journal writer's job is.

83

Unit 6

Review Words

A. Check the words you know.

☐ **1.** picked   ☐ **2.** here   ☐ **3.** sweeping

☐ **4.** if   ☐ **5.** been   ☐ **6.** before

☐ **7.** cooking   ☐ **8.** then   ☐ **9.** sentence

☐ **10.** year   ☐ **11.** blues   ☐ **12.** thinking

B. Read and write the sentences. Circle the review words.

1. Pam stopped sweeping and cooking for a minute.

_____

_____

2. Then she picked up the card from Rose.

_____

3. The last sentence said, "I've got the blues because I've been thinking of you."

_____

_____

4. Pam would be so glad if Rose could come to see her before this year is over.

_____

_____

C. Read the clues. Write the opposite of each clue in the puzzle.

Down
1. there

Across
2. after
3. now

Instructor's Notes: Read each set of directions with students. For A, have students read the words aloud and then check known words. Have students practice any unknown words in a notebook or journal.

84

Unit 6

Sight Words

visit • permission
immigration • green

A. Read the words above. Then read the sentences.

Rose can **visit**, but she wants **permission** to work here.
Immigration laws say she must get a **green** card.

B. Underline the sight words in sentences 1–5.

1. I know about the immigration laws here.

2. It took me a long time to get my own green card.

3. Rose doesn't need permission to visit me.

4. If Rose wanted to work here, she would have to get a green card.

5. The immigration laws try to keep newcomers from taking work that people here could do.

C. Write the word that best completes each sentence.

immigration   visit   permission   green

1. My island country is very _____ with lots of grass and trees.

2. I would like to go _____ my family.

3. There aren't many jobs on my island, so I got _____ to work here.

4. It's hard to meet the _____ laws.

D. Read the sentences. Underline the sight words.

When I first wanted to come to this country, I didn't know much about the immigration laws. I waited to get my green card so I would have permission to work for the Prices. Getting a green card is much harder than coming here to visit.

Instructor's Notes: Read each set of directions with students. For A, read each sight word aloud and have students repeat it.

Sight Words
American ● employer
goes ● house

A. Read the words above. Then read the sentence.

My **American employer goes** out to work, and I work in the **house**.

B. Underline the sight words in sentences 1–4.

1. I keep house for my American employers.

2. I do the best I can with their house and the children.

3. The Prices gave me a responsible job and a small room in their house.

4. Some of the money I make goes to help my family back home.

C. Write the word that best completes each sentence.

    American   employers   goes   house

1. Some of my pay _____ to my family back home in the islands.

2. In many _____ families, both parents work.

3. These parents need someone to keep the _____ and babysit with the kids.

4. I was lucky to find nice _____ .

D. Read the sentences. Underline the sight words.

   The American immigration laws say I must have a green card to work in this country. Not many Americans want to be a housekeeper, so this kind of job goes to people like me. I'm lucky because the Prices are good employers.

Instructor's Notes: Read each set of directions with students. For A, read each sight word aloud and have students repeat it. Discuss with students that words that name a nationality, like *American*, are capitalized.

Sight Words
call ● legal
draw ● papers

A. Read the words above. Then read the sentence.

I had to **call** on **legal** help to **draw** up the **papers** I needed for the immigration people.

B. Underline the sight words in sentences 1–4.

1. I needed legal help to get a green card.

2. Getting a green card takes time, money, and many calls, letters, and legal papers.

3. I had to draw money out of my savings to pay for the legal costs.

4. The immigration people checked to see that the legal papers were right.

C. Write the word that best completes each sentence.

called   draw   legal   papers

1. The _____ costs for a green card are pretty high.

2. I never saw so many _____ !

3. It takes a lot of time to _____ up so many papers.

4. I _____ many people for help.

D. Read the sentences. Underline the sight words.

Every day when Ike and Shelly come home from school, they call their mother at her job. Then they show me their drawings and school papers. We laugh and kid around. This draws my thoughts away from Rose and my island home. It's nice not to have legal papers to worry about anymore.

Instructor's Notes: Read each set of directions with students. For A, read each sight word aloud and have students repeat it. For D, point out that the *s* in *island* is silent. Encourage students to practice writing sentences from Review Word and Sight Word pages in a notebook or journal.

87

Unit 6

Phonics   -all and -aw

A. Read the words on the left. Write other -all words.

-all
call
ball
fall

t   + all = _____

w + all = _____

sm + all = _____

B. Write an -all word to finish each sentence.

1. I've spent hours trying to _____ the immigration people about my sister.

2. A _____ man with a kind look told me all the immigration rules.

3. When I met with them, they put me in a _____ room with lots of other people.

C. Read the words on the left. Write other -aw words.

-aw
law
jaw
saw

p   + aw = _____

fl   + aw = _____

dr + aw = _____

str + aw = _____

D. Write an -aw word to finish each sentence.

1. It's hard for a person to know everything about immigration

_____ .

2. I needed legal help to _____ up the papers.

3. They'll send the papers back to you if they find a

_____ in them.

Instructor's Notes: Show students the -all word pattern in the known sight word call. Discuss with students that the a in these words stands for a special vowel sound, neither long nor short. Then read each set of directions with students. Repeat for the -aw pattern.

Phonics   Syllables and Schwa

A. Listen for the number of word parts you hear in each word below. Each part is called a syllable, and each syllable has one vowel sound.

1 Syllable	2 Syllables	3 Syllables	4 Syllables
best	pa-pers	u-ni-form	A-mer-i-cans
spoil	le-gal	fur-ni-ture	Feb-ru-ar-y
threw	pro-gram	an-oth-er	im-mi-gra-tion

B. Listen for how many syllables you hear in each word below. Write the number.

parent _____   credit _____

responsible _____   newcomer _____

arrested _____   strain _____

C. Listen for the vowel sound in the underlined syllables below. This vowel sound is called the schwa. Each of the vowels <u>a</u>, <u>e</u>, <u>i</u>, <u>o</u>, or <u>u</u> can stand for the schwa sound.

a	**e**	**i**	**o**	**u**
<u>a</u>-lone	par-<u>ent</u>	fam-<u>i</u>-ly	per-<u>son</u>	help-<u>ful</u>

D. Listen for the schwa sound in the words below. Write the letter that stands for the schwa sound.

about _____   sentence _____   doctor _____

April _____   actor _____   August _____

E. Choose a word from part A above to complete each sentence.

1. Most of my family live in _____ country.

2. They would like to come here and become _____ .

3. They will need to have all their _____ in order.

Instructor's Notes: For A and C, read the explanation and the sample words. Have students repeat the words. For B and D, read the directions and the words. Have students repeat the words. For E, read the directions with students.

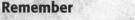

Remember
What has happened in the story
so far?

Predict
What do you think will happen in
the rest of the story?

A Home Away From Home

September 2

Rose came to visit, and we had the best time! She got along very well with the Prices, and they really liked her. They gave me as much time off work as they could so Rose and I could be together. I think they knew that I had been homesick for many months.

Shelly and Ike loved Rose, too. They were always giving her their drawings. The four of us played a lot of games in my room. How we laughed! I remember when Mrs. Price's friend, Mrs. Brown, came over. She came in to see what we were laughing about and pretty soon she was laughing, too. Now Rose is back in the islands and I'm lonely again.

September 30

The mail came, and I got a letter from Rose today. She said that she had the best time on her visit. She said, too, that she really liked this country. Before her visit, she didn't think she would like it here. I wish she were here now.

October 10

What good news! Mrs. Brown came over today to tell us that she's pregnant. But that's not all! Mrs. Brown wants Rose to work for her if Rose can get a green card. Then Rose can stay with the baby when Mrs. Brown goes back to work. I hope it works out!

Instructor's Notes: Read the questions with students. Help students review and predict.
Then have students read the story silently.

90

Unit 6

October 18

Mrs. Price helped me write to Rose. I told her about Mrs. Brown's baby and that she would like Rose to come and work for her. I told Rose she would have to get a green card, like I did, and that it might take a long time.

November 8

Mrs. Brown was here again. When her baby comes in June, Mrs. Brown will take six months off from work. I don't think Rose will have her green card by the time Mrs. Brown goes back to work. What will happen then? Will Mrs. Brown find another woman to look after the new baby?

November 13

Rose wrote to me and to Mrs. Brown, too. She wants very much to get her green card and come here to work. It may take two years, but it's something we can all work for.

December 5

It's a good thing that Rose had a housekeeping job in the islands because she must show immigration that she has housekeeping skills. Mrs. Brown must show that she ran ads and cannot find an American to do this job. I worry that she might find someone and Rose won't get her green card.

June 17

The Browns had a boy! I'll write to Rose about him.

July 30

I'm a little worried. Mrs. Brown says she likes being at home with the baby. What if she doesn't go back to work? What if she doesn't need Rose? Then my sister won't have a job.

November 19

Mrs. Brown is going back to work in January, but Rose still doesn't have her green card. I don't know how this will end. I'm very worried.

December 11

Mrs. Brown now plans to go back to work only part-time. She and Mr. Brown will plan their work schedules so that one of them will always be at home with the baby. This will be hard, but they're willing to wait for Rose to get her green card.

September 24

It's been a long year and a lot of hard work, but it's paying off. The immigration people say Rose will be getting her green card soon. Maybe by the end of this year. What a party we'll have then! I don't know which one of us will feel luckier— Rose or Mrs. Brown or baby Tim or me.

Comprehension

Think About It

1. Why was Pam homesick?

2. How did she help Rose get a job?

3. Sum up what happened in the story.

Write About It

What do you think about immigration laws?

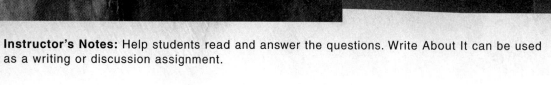

Instructor's Notes: Help students read and answer the questions. Write About It can be used as a writing or discussion assignment.

Drawing Conclusions

A **conclusion** is an opinion or judgment you make after studying all the facts you have. The conclusion is usually not stated directly in what you read. You draw a conclusion based on what you know and what you have learned by reading. You have to read between the lines to draw a conclusion.

Use these tips to draw a conclusion:

1. Read the paragraph or story.

2. Recall or list all the facts.

3. Think about the facts. Then read between the lines.

4. Draw a conclusion. (Check yourself by asking if the facts support your conclusion.)

A. Decide what conclusions you can draw from the story on pages 82–83 and 90–92. Circle the letter for the correct answer.

1. You can conclude that Pam
   a. wants to find another job.
   b. likes it here and plans to stay.
   c. doesn't get along with her employer.

2. You can conclude that the Prices
   a. want to keep Pam as their housekeeper.
   b. work for the immigration people.
   c. want Rose to work for them.

3. You can conclude that a green card is
   a. for American workers.
   b. hard for newcomers to get.
   c. only for employers.

4. You can conclude that Mrs. Brown
   a. didn't think very highly of Pam.
   b. didn't remember what Rose was like.
   c. thought Rose would be a good worker.

Instructor's Notes: Discuss the tips with students. Explain the phrase *to read between the lines*. Then read the directions for the exercise together.

Add -ed to some verbs to show the past. For other words, change the spelling to show the past.

drive drove   run ran

Example: I drive a car. (I am doing it <u>now</u>.)

I drove a car. (I did it in the <u>past</u>.)

A. Read this list of verbs.

Present	Past	Present	Past
keep	kept	write	wrote
draw	drew	think	thought
bring	brought	eat	ate
drive	drove	fight	fought
sweep	swept	swim	swam

B. Read the paragraph. Underline the verbs that show the past.

Rose wrote to Pam. Rose told about the legal work she was doing to get her green card. She brought her problems to a woman who drew up the papers she needed. Rose knew it would take a long time to get the green card. She fought hard not to get upset or give up trying.

C. Choose the verb that tells about the past. Write it in the sentence.

1. Ike and Shelly _____ the food Pam cooked.

   ate   eat

2. Pam _____ and cleaned the house each week.

   sweep   swept

3. When Pam lived in the islands, she _____ in the blue water.

   swam   swim

Instructor's Notes: Discuss with students that some verbs show past tense by changing spelling rather than by adding -ed. Read the examples aloud. For A, read each present tense verb aloud to students and have them read the past tense aloud. Read each set of directions with students.

94

Unit 6

D. Write the missing present or past form of each verb.

1. kept _____

2. knew _____

3. fight _____

4. swam _____

5. drove _____

6. eat _____

7. bring _____

8. swept _____

E. Read the sentences. Underline the sentence in each pair that has a verb with an irregular past form.

1. Rose wanted her green card.

   Rose wrote about her green card.

2. Pam knew the Brown family.

   Pam worked for the Prices.

3. Mrs. Brown drove Pam to the store.

   Mrs. Brown helped Pam with the food.

F. Write three sentences of your own. Use an irregular past tense verb in each sentence.

1. _____

   _____

2. _____

   _____

3. _____

   _____

Instructor's Notes: Read each set of directions with students. For D, have students tell if the word they write is the present or past tense form. For F, discuss with students the sentences and verb forms they will write.

Filling Out a Form

middle   form   information   male   female

A. Read the words. Then read the form. A person who is trying to get a green card might fill out a form like this.

Immigration and Naturalization Service **BIOGRAPHIC INFORMATION** No. 1115-0066

1	(Family Name)　　(First Name)　　(Middle name)	☐ MALE ☐ FEMALE	BIRTHDATE (Mo.-Day-Yr.)	NATIONALITY	FILE NUMBER A-
2	ALL OTHER NAMES USED (including names by previous marriages)	CITY AND COUNTRY OF BIRTH			SOCIAL SECURITY NO.

	FAMILY NAME　FIRST NAME　DATE, CITY AND COUNTRY OF BIRTH (If known)　CITY AND COUNTRY OF RESIDENCE.
3	FATHER MOTHER (Maiden name)

	HUSBAND (If none, so state) OR WIFE	FAMILY NAME (For wife, give maiden name)	FIRST NAME	BIRTHDATE	CITY & COUNTRY OF BIRTH	DATE OF MARRIAGE	PLACE OF MARRIAGE
4							

5	FORMER HUSBANDS OR WIVES (if none, so state)				
	FAMILY NAME (For wife, give maiden name)	FIRST NAME	BIRTHDATE	DATE & PLACE OF MARRIAGE	DATE AND PLACE OF TERMINATION OF MARRIAGE

APPLICANT'S RESIDENCE LAST FIVE YEARS. LIST PRESENT ADDRESS FIRST.

6	STREET AND NUMBER	CITY	PROVINCE OR STATE	COUNTRY	FROM MONTH	FROM YEAR	TO MONTH	TO YEAR
							PRESENT TIME	

B. Read the questions and write the answers.

1. Would Rose write the word <u>Rose</u> as her family name, first name,

   or middle name on the form? _____

2. On which line would Rose give information about her parents?

   _____

3. Would Rose check male or female on the form? _____

4. On which line of the form would Rose give information about

   where she lives? _____

Instructor's Notes: Read the new words and each set of directions with students. Help them read the form and answer the questions. Use the Unit 6 Review on page 97 to conclude the unit. Then assign *Reading for Today Workbook Five*, Unit 6.

Unit 6 Review

A. Write the word that best completes each sentence.

call	legal	green	employer
goes	visit	papers	permission
draw	house	American	immigration

1. Pam knew a lot about _____ laws.

2. Rose came to America to _____ her sister.

3. Now Rose would like _____ to work in America.

4. She will need legal help to get a _____ card.

B. Write -all or -aw to make new words. Write each word in a sentence.

1. s + _____ = _____   When Rose _____ America, she wanted to live here.

2. sm + _____ = _____   Rose could get a job working with

_____ children.

3. c + _____ = _____   Pam will _____ the immigration people.

4. l + _____ = _____   The _____ says that Rose must get a green card.

C. Choose the verb that tells about the past. Write it in the sentence.

1. Rose _____ a long letter to Pam.
   write   wrote

2. Pam _____ the letter to read again later.
   kept   keep

3. She _____ back the tears as she thought of her sister.
   fought   fight

4. Pam _____ it would be a long time before she saw Rose again.
   know   knew

Discussion

Remember
Look at the picture. What do you think is happening? Have you or a friend ever been in this situation?

Predict
Look at the picture and the title. What do you think this story is about?

Will They Meet?

Pedro stopped at the card shop on his way home from work. He still had his work uniform on and it wasn't very clean, but he planned to get in and out of the shop before anyone saw him. He just needed a get-well card for a friend. If he got the card now, he wouldn't have to worry about it again.

There were lots of people in the shop, but Pedro had no trouble slipping to the back. The real problem was picking a card to buy. Pedro couldn't make up his mind. He was just about to pick a big green one when something made him look up. It wasn't something. It was someone—the best-looking someone in all the city. Pedro forgot what he had been doing. He could only stand there looking at her.

"Could I get by you?" a man asked. "I'd like to look at those cards."

Pedro let the man go by. Then he walked around the shop. He just had to find out who she was. What was her name? Did she work here? How could he get to know her? She was walking around the store looking at the cards. Pedro picked up the green card again and went to pay for it. He hoped she would come over to take his money, but he wasn't so lucky.

The story continues.

Instructor's Notes: Read the discussion questions with students. Discuss the story title and the situation in the picture. Have students read silently. Have them underline words they don't recognize. Review the underlined words. Have students identify the characters.

99

Unit 7

Review Words

A. Check the words you know.

☐ **1.** saw   ☐ **2.** must   ☐ **3.** summer

☐ **4.** how   ☐ **5.** soon   ☐ **6.** thank

☐ **7.** too   ☐ **8.** ask   ☐ **9.** would

☐ **10.** why   ☐ **11.** card   ☐ **12.** better

B. Read and write the sentences. Circle the review words.

1. Pedro saw someone at the card shop who he would like to know better.

_____

_____

2. How would he talk to someone who was so pretty?

_____

_____

3. Why was he too shy to ask her for a date?

_____

_____

C. Read the clues. Complete the puzzle.

Across
1. the part of the year that comes after spring
3. Tell someone you are glad for the help.

Down
1. right away
2. need to or have to

Instructor's Notes: Read each set of directions with students. For A, have students read the words and then check known words. Have students practice any unknown words in a notebook or journal.

Sight Words

noticed ● girl
start ● true

A. Read the words above. Then read the sentences.

Pedro **noticed** the **girl** right from the **start**. "I think I've found my **true** love!" he said.

B. Underline the sight words in sentences 1–5.

1. Pedro noticed the girl right away.

2. Seeing her for the first time gave him a start.

3. She was too good to be true!

4. Pedro didn't know if the girl noticed him.

5. He wanted to say something, but he didn't know where to start.

C. Write the word that best completes each sentence.

girl   true   started   notice

1. Pedro _____ to pay for his card.

2. He hoped to meet the _____ .

3. Would she _____ him standing there?

4. Was it _____ that she worked in the card shop?

D. Read the sentences. Underline the sight words.

Pedro couldn't get the girl from the card shop out of his mind. He started thinking about how he could meet her. He would go back to the shop and get her to notice him. It was true that he didn't need more cards, but he would go back to the shop anyway.

Instructor's Notes: Read each set of directions with students. For A, read each sight word aloud and have students repeat it.

Sight Words

idea • few
birthday • open

A. Read the words above. Then read the sentence.

Pedro's **idea** was to look for a **few birthday** cards if the shop was **open**.

B. Underline the sight words in sentences 1–4.

1. Pedro's idea was to go back to the shop soon.

2. He would look at the birthday cards this time.

3. The shop was open, but only a few people were there.

4. Pedro had no idea what to say to the girl.

C. Write the word that best completes each sentence.

birthday   open   few   ideas

1. Pedro looked at a _____ cards.

2. Some of the _____ in them were pretty good.

3. Pedro did not know anyone who was having a _____ anytime soon.

4. Pedro saw the girl _____ a card and show it to a customer.

D. Read the sentences. Underline the sight words.

Pedro opened one card after another. Soon he would have to buy a few. The girl would get the wrong idea if he didn't buy some, so he picked out a few birthday cards and went to her. When he tried to pay her, he dropped his money. The girl didn't say anything, but Pedro got the idea that she must be laughing at him.

Instructor's Notes: Read each set of directions with students. For A, read each sight word aloud and have students repeat it.

102

Unit 7

Sight Words
wish ● please
far ● warm

A. Read the words above. Then read the sentences.

Pedro's **wish** was to **please** the girl, but he didn't get very **far**.
Her look was not **warm**.

B. Underline the sight words in sentences 1–5.

1. Pedro wished to talk to the girl, but he was shy.

2. "Please tell me your name," he asked.

3. He learned that her name was Ana, but still he was far from asking her out.

4. "Please tell me why you buy so many cards," she said.

5. Pedro started to feel warm all over and forgot what he wanted to say.

C. Write the word that best completes each sentence.

warmly   pleased   far   wished

1. Pedro _____ that he could tell Ana the real story.

2. He hoped that she would act _____ to him.

3. Would she be _____ that he liked her?

4. How _____ would he go to get Ana interested in him?

D. Read the sentences. Underline the sight words.

Pedro wasn't too pleased about buying so many cards. "I wish I could think of another way to see Ana," he thought. "She doesn't know me, so I won't get too far if I just ask her out. I wish I could get her to warm up to the idea of a date."

Instructor's Notes: Read each set of directions with students. For A, read each sight word aloud. Have students repeat. Discuss with students that *warm* can be used in more than one way. Have students practice writing sentences from Review Word and Sight Word pages in a notebook or journal.

-ue and -ew

-ue

true

blue

due

A. Read the words on the left. Write other -ue words.

cl + ue = _____

fl + ue = _____

gl + ue = _____

B. Write a -ue word to finish each sentence.

1. It's _____ that Pedro wanted Ana to notice him.

2. He picked out a _____ and green birthday card in the shop.

3. He has many other cards, but he doesn't have a _____ about what they say.

4. Sometimes Pedro can't spend much time at the card shop because

   he is _____ back at work.

-ew

few

grew

new

C. Read the words on the left. Write other -ew words.

ch + ew = _____

fl + ew = _____

cr + ew = _____

thr + ew = _____

D. Write an -ew word to finish each sentence.

1. Pedro _____ very shy when Ana looked at him.

2. He went back to the shop and got a _____ more cards.

3. He _____ out many cards that he would never use.

4. Pedro hoped Ana would be a _____ friend.

Instructor's Notes: Show students the *-ue* pattern in the known sight word *true*. Then read
each set of directions with students. Repeat these steps for the *-ew* pattern. Explain that *-ue*
and *-ew* stand for the same vowel sound in these words.

A. The letters oo can stand for the long vowel sound heard in food. The letters ue, ew, and ou can stand for the same sound. Underline the vowels below.

o͞o	ue	ew	ou
food	blue	blew	group
mood	clue	chew	soup

B. Make other words with o͞o.

m + oon= _____   c + ool = _____

n + oon= _____   p + ool = _____

sw + oon= _____   st + ool = _____

C. The letters o͝o can stand for the short vowel sound heard in good. The letters ou can also stand for this sound. Underline the vowels below.

o͝o		ou	
good	hood	could	should
wood	stood	would	

D. Make other words with o͝o.

b + ook= _____   br + ook= _____

c + ook= _____   cr + ook= _____

h + ook= _____   sh + ook= _____

E. Choose a word from above to complete each sentence.

1. Pedro tried to be _____ when he talked to Ana, but he grew warm.

2. Pedro was so shy around Ana that his hand _____ .

Instructor's Notes: For A and C, read the words aloud and have students repeat them. Read each set of directions with students.

Remember
What has happened in the story
so far?

Predict
What do you think will happen in
the rest of the story?

Will They Meet?

Pedro sat in his room talking to himself about Ana. Just going into the shop and buying cards wasn't doing him much good. Ana noticed that he had picked out a lot of birthday cards, but she didn't notice him. To Ana, he was only a customer who came into the shop.

"She must have a boyfriend," Pedro said to himself. He didn't like to think about that problem.

"Could I call her?" he asked himself. "No! She doesn't know my name."

"Will it do any good to buy more cards?" he thought. "No! She just tells me the price and takes my money. I can't afford to spend all my money on cards!"

Pedro picked up a card with blue, green, and red stars. "Cute," said Pedro, "but what will I do with it?"

Then Pedro got his bright idea. At first he liked the idea. "Why not?" he asked himself. Then he didn't like it. "Who am I kidding?" he said. Then he liked it again. "I'll try it!" he cried. "After all, what can I lose?"

So Pedro got a pen and sat down at his table. He opened the card and started to write.

After work on Monday, Pedro went back to the card shop once more. This time he didn't buy anything. He went straight to where Ana was working and saw she was alone. Good! He didn't want to get Ana in trouble with her boss. Pedro gave her the card.

"It's for you," he said. "I picked it out myself."

Instructor's Notes: Read the questions with students. Help students review and predict. Then have students read the story silently.

106

Unit 7

Ana looked up. "For me?" she asked. "Why?" She started to open the card. Pedro grew worried. What was she going to think?

Ana looked at the card, then at Pedro. "Thanks," she said, "but why are you giving me a card?"

Pedro looked down at the ground. "Well, I just wanted to thank you for being so nice to me," he said.

Ana laughed warmly. "But why are you giving a card to someone you don't know? I thought you sent all those cards to your friends in faraway towns."

Pedro didn't know what to answer, but he had to come up with something. After all, she was talking to him. He grew warm at the thought. She was talking to him!

"I do, but I like to have friends here, too," he said.

Ana grinned. "That's very nice," she said. "It's a little strange, but nice." After a few minutes she said, "It's no fun to sell cards if you don't get any."

Pedro was pleased. This was a good start!

"Now I know your name," said Ana, "because it's on the card. I didn't know how to find out who you are. You always get so red when I look at you. Pedro is a nice name. I like it."

Pedro got very red.

"Listen," Ana went on, "if we're going to be friends, we need to know more about one another. I get off work soon. Can you stay around?"

Pedro grinned. "You bet!" he said. "I'll just look at the cards."

Ana winked at him and said, "Don't tell me you need more cards. You must have cards all over your house."

Pedro laughed at that. "It's true! I could open a card store myself, but then I wouldn't get to see you," he said boldly. He didn't feel so shy anymore. Ana was fun to talk to, and she was very open.

Pedro went around to a small card rack that he had noticed a few days before. He had lots of birthday cards and holiday cards, but there was one kind of card he didn't have. He looked for just the right one. This one? No, that was too plain. That one? Then Pedro saw the card he wanted. "That will do very well," he thought. "I hope I'll need it soon."

Pedro slipped the card in a bag so Ana wouldn't see it. He didn't want her to see it just yet, so he told her how much it cost and paid for it. He waited while Ana locked up the card shop.

Then he and Ana walked over to a snack shop where they sat together at a small table and talked for a long time. Pedro's newest card, the one that said "I love you," was in the bag on the table. Some day, not yet, he might give it to Ana.

Comprehension

Think About It

1. Why was Pedro afraid to call Ana at first?
2. How did he get Ana to pay attention to him?
3. What happened after Pedro gave Ana a card?
4. Sum up what happened in the story.

Write About It

Have you ever been in a situation where you wanted to meet someone? What did you do?

Instructor's Notes: Help students read and answer the questions. Write About It can be used as a writing or discussion assignment.

108

Unit 7

 **Comprehension**   **Classifying**

When you classify things, you put them in groups with other things they are like. For example, Ana might classify her customers into these groups:

Men   Women   Children

Use these tips when you want to classify information you read.

1. Read the paragraph or story.

2. Look for ways that things are alike.

3. List headings for different groups of facts or ideas.

4. Put the facts or ideas under the best headings.

A. Read the paragraph.

Pedro had three get-well cards. One showed a nurse, and the others both had cats on them. His birthday cards had dogs, flags, kites, and lots of other things on them.

B. Underline the best headings.

1. Dogs and Cats

2. Get-Well Cards and Birthday Cards

3. Animals and People

C. Put ideas from the paragraph under the headings you chose.

_____   _____

_____   _____

_____   _____

_____   _____

_____   _____

Instructor's Notes: Read the tips aloud with students. Discuss classifying as a process of sorting things into groups based on likeness. Then read the directions with students and help them do the exercises.

Reflexive Pronouns ▬▬▬▬▬▬

> Pronouns made with **-self** or **-selves** are called **reflexive pronouns**.
> my + self = myself   them + selves = themselves

A. Add the word self to the words you already know to make new words. Then write the word.

1. him + _____ = _____

2. her + _____ = _____

3. your + _____ = _____

4. my   + _____ = _____

B. The plural of self is selves. Add -selves to these words.

1. your + _____ = _____

2. them + _____ = _____

3. our + _____ = _____

C. Choose the correct pronoun. Write it in the sentence.

1. "Can you put out all those cards by _____ or do you need some help?"
   yourself   himself

2. Ana and her helper could do the work _____ , so their boss went to see a customer.
   themselves   myself

3. "We can do this _____ in about an hour," Ana told her helper.
   myself   ourselves

4. Ana liked to work by _____ best.
   yourself   herself

5. Ana said, "I will do this job _____ ."
   myself   yourself

Instructor's Notes: Discuss with students: suffix *-self* can be added to the pronouns *him, her, my, your,* and its plural *-selves* can be added to *our, your, them.* Read each set of directions with students.

D. Read the paragraphs. Underline the reflexive pronouns.

On Monday Ana was by herself in the store. "There are not so many customers now, so I can work by myself," she said. "Most people help themselves when it comes to buying cards."

On Tuesday Pedro came in by himself. He looked at the cards by himself for a long time. When he brought a card for Ana to ring up, she said, "You bought yourself a good card. I like that one."

Pedro's eyes lit up. "Thanks!" he said. As he opened the door, he turned and said, "Take care of yourself now."

E. Underline the mistake in each sentence. Write the sentence correctly.

1. "We can open up the shop yourselves," Ana told her helper.

   _____

2. Ana said, "I, herself, need to write some checks."

   _____

3. A customer talked to themselves as he picked out a card.

   _____

F. Write three of your own sentences. Use a reflexive pronoun in each sentence.

1. _____

   _____

2. _____

   _____

3. _____

   _____

Instructor's Notes: Read each set of directions to students. For F, discuss with students their sentences and the reflexive pronouns they will use.

111

Unit 7

menu   extras   least   beverages

A. Read the words above. Then read the menu.

Eats Cafe

SANDWICHES

WHITE OR WHOLE WHEAT

SERVED WITH ONE EXTRA

Turkey	$ 3.50
Ham and Cheese	$ 3.75
Chicken Salad	$ 3.50
Tuna Salad	$ 3.25
Grilled Cheese	$ 3.00
Bacon, Lettuce and Tomato	$ 3.75
Egg Salad	$ 3.00

DIET DELIGHT

Cottage cheese, fruit, and veggies	$ 4.95

GRILL

SERVED WITH CHOICE OF TWO EXTRAS

Shrimp	$10.95
Filet Mignon	$ 7.95
Sirloin	$ 7.95
Chopped Steak	$ 5.25
Grilled Chicken	$ 6.50
Hamburger	$ 4.50
Cheeseburger	$ 4.75

DINNER SALAD

Blue Cheese, Creamy Herb, or Ranch	$ 1.50

BEVERAGES

Cold drinks	$ .95
Lemonade	$ .95
Fruit juice	$ .95
Milk	$ .95
Coffee	$ .75
Tea	$ .75

DESSERTS

Pies: apple, blueberry, lemon	$ 2.50
Chocolate Cake	$ 3.00
Vanilla Custard	$ 2.50
Ice Cream (Ask for today's flavors)	$ 2.00

EXTRAS $1.50

Baked Potato	French Fries
Rice	Onion Rings
Potato Salad	Beans
Cole Slaw	

B. Read the questions and write the answers.

1. **a.** What foods on the menu cost the least, other than the beverages?

   _____

   b. What food costs the most? _____

2. If you want a cold drink, what heading should you look under?

   _____

3. You have $6.00 to spend on lunch. What will you order?

   _____

Instructor's Notes: Read the new words and each set of directions with students. Help them read the menu and answer the questions. Use the Unit 7 Review on page 113 to conclude the unit. Then assign *Reading for Today Workbook Five*, Unit 7. Use Blackline Master 8: Certificate of Completion from the *Instructor's Guide* to recognize students who successfully complete this book.

A. Write the word that best completes each sentence.

girl	far	idea	noticed
few	true	open	please
wished	warm	start	birthday

1. Pedro liked the _____ of getting to know Ana.

2. He _____ that he could think of a way to meet her.

3. He hoped that giving Ana a card would _____ her.

4. Ana _____ that Pedro was very shy around her.

B. Write -ue or -ew to make new words. Write each word in a sentence.

1. bl + _____ = _____ Pedro was feeling pretty _____ .

2. cl + _____ = _____ He didn't have a _____ about how to please Ana.

3. n + _____ = _____ He bought a _____ card for Ana.

4. gr + _____ = _____ Pedro _____ bolder after Ana talked to him.

C. Choose the correct pronoun. Write it in the sentence.

1. Pedro asked _____ what to do to meet Ana.
   himself   myself

2. "If she walks home by _____ , she might want some company,"
   he thought.   themselves   herself

3. "Do you want to be by _____ ?" he asked shyly.
   himself   yourself

4. "I was going to walk home by _____ ," Ana said, "but I would
   like it if you walked with me."   myself   ourselves

A. Write the words that best complete each sentence.

decided	business	building	possible
worn	under	furniture	interest
afford	credit	plain	check

1. I live in a _____ that has big rooms.

2. I like to fix _____ that is _____ out.

3. Was it _____ to make a _____ out of this?

4. I _____ to give it a try.

5. I can _____ to take a chance.

6. People can pay me by _____ card or by _____ .

B. Write -ark, -ain, -ice, or -ive to make new words. Write the word that fits best in the sentence.

1. p + _____ = _____ I walk in the _____ .

2. str + _____ = _____ It's a _____ to live like this.

3. n + _____ = _____ I need a _____ job.

4. f + _____ = _____ I need _____ people to help.

C. Classify the words. Write them under the correct headings.

meat	pants	rice	house	apartment
socks	hat	hut	milk	

Food	Homes	Clothes
_____	_____	_____
_____	_____	_____
_____	_____	_____

D. Add -es, -ed, -'s or -s'. Write the word in the sentence.

1. (-es)   Lin _____ about her family.
                         worry

2. (-'s)   Her _____ health is not good.
                     mother

3. (-ed)   The children _____ when she got there.
                            cry

4. (-s')   Her two _____ pay checks had not come in.
                     brother

E. Choose the correct word. Write it in the sentence.

1. He is the _____ of the three children.
                smaller   smallest

2. His room is the _____ one in the house.
                   cleanest   cleaner

3. He is much _____ than his brother.
                  neater   neatest

F. Write the word that best completes each sentence.

only	instrument	popular	styles
show	any	musician	town

1. Music is very _____ in our little _____ .

2. That _____ doesn't like to play alone.

3. The _____ I play is the guitar.

4. I can _____ you how to play it.

5. You can play in the band _____ time you like.

6. We play different _____ of music.

G. Write -ound, -own, -oil, or -oy to make new words. Write the word that fits best in the sentence.

1. t + _____ = _____ We went to _____ to shop.

2. sp + _____ = _____ The rain didn't _____ our day.

3. ar + _____ = _____ We looked _____ in the stores.

4. t + _____ = _____ I bought a _____ for my child.

5. j + _____ = _____ It will bring her a lot of _____ .

6. f + _____ = _____ I was glad when I _____ it.

H. Write the word that best completes each sentence.

famous	answer	success	those
visit	American	papers	employer
noticed	true	please	idea

1. Mrs. Lin is my _____ .

2. Her business is a big _____ .

3. We all _____ her name in the papers.

4. She is _____ for helping her workers.

5. A new _____ can find a job in her store.

6. We think of her as a _____ friend.

7. We all work hard to _____ her.

8. She wants to hear any new _____ we have for doing our jobs.

I. Write the verb that tells about the past.

1. Ted _____ a letter to his mother.
   write   wrote

2. She _____ it to show to Roy.
   kept   keep

3. The two boys sometimes _____ .
   fought   fight

4. Ted _____ this upset everyone.
   know   knew

J. Write -all, -aw, -ue, or -ew to make new words. Write the word that best completes the sentence.

1. n + _____ = _____ They love their _____ home.

2. h + _____ = _____ The _____ is big and bright.

3. s + _____ = _____ I _____ a picture of it.

4. bl + _____ = _____ I painted the house _____ .

K. Write the correct reflexive pronoun.

1. She wrote this story _____ .
   myself   herself

2. I can see _____ in it.
   themselves   myself

3. Here, read it for _____ .
   yourself   himself

4. We should write some stories _____ .
   myself   ourselves

Ode to Mi Gato

He's white
As spilled milk,
My cat who sleeps
With his belly
Turned toward
The summer sky.
He loves the sun,
Its warmth like a hand.
He loves tuna cans
And milk cartons
With their dribble
Of milk. He loves
Mom when she rattles
The bag of cat food,
The brown nuggets
Raining into his bowl.
And my cat loves
Me, because I saved
Him from a dog,
Because I dressed him
In a hat and a cape
For Halloween,
Because I dangled
A sock of chicken skin
As he stood on his
Hind legs. I love mi gato,
Porque I found
Him on the fender

Of an abandoned car.
He was a kitten
With a meow
Like the rusty latch
On a gate. I carried
Him home in the loop
Of my arms.
I poured milk
Into him, let him
Lick chunks of
Cheese from my palms,
And cooked huevo
After huevo
Until his purring
Engine kicked in
And he cuddled
Up to my father's slippers.
That was last year.
This spring,
He's excellent at sleeping
And no good
At hunting. At night
All the other cats
In the neighborhood
Can see him slink
Around the corner,
Or jump from the tree
Like a splash of
Milk. We lap up
His love and
He laps up his welcome.

by Gary Soto

What Do You Think?

**Do you have a pet?
Is it important to you?**

Pets and People

Are you feeling under the weather? A Siamese or a Chihuahua might do you as much good as a pill. Studies have shown that pets can improve your health. In fact, elderly people with pets go to the doctor less frequently than those without pets. Pets can even make a life or death difference for people who have had heart surgery—those with pets survive longer. Scientists are still trying to discover exactly how pets affect health. Pet owners know, though, that companion animals can help them feel better emotionally and physically.

Has your dog ever said you were messy or lazy? Does your cat criticize your clothes? Animals are never critical. Animals accept people just as they are. This makes them relaxing companions. Susanne Robb found that nursing home patients who were visited regularly by pets smiled more and were more alert. The presence of animals has also been shown to calm people who have trouble getting along with others. In addition to calming our emotions, pets can actually calm our bodies. Erika Friedmann of Brooklyn College found that people's heart rates are even lower when they are with a pet than when they are alone.

Another way that pets improve people's health is by providing an opportunity to be responsible. Taking care of an animal can help people feel important and successful. If you've ever taken a sad, scrawny animal home from the animal shelter and watched it become a sleek, happy member of the family, you know how powerful the effect of caring for a pet can be. Green Chimneys Children's Shelter in Brewster, New York, helps children overcome their difficulties by allowing them to take care of farm animals or work in a wildlife rehabilitation program. The success of such programs has helped the use of pets as therapy to gain acceptance.

While pet therapy will never replace other medical treatments, it can certainly complement them. Most important, pets can help keep you from getting sick in the first place—without side effects! So eat your vegetables, get plenty of exercise, and spend some time with your favorite animal.

Unit 1

Page 4

A. Answers will vary.

B. 1. The (company) had to let April and the (other) workers go.

2. (How) many (days) will it be before she can (find) a (new) job?

3. She will look (around) for work (because) she is (responsible) for (her) (family).

C. 1. line to before; after

2. line to lose; find

3. line to him; her

4. line to night; day

5. line to old; new

Page 5

B. 1. Could April find work in the same business?

2. Would it be better to work in a different business?

3. How fast is it possible to find a new job?

4. April decided to find out.

C. 1. possible 2. business 3. fast 4. decided

D. "What work can I do?" asked April. "Maybe I can go into a different business." She wanted a job fast, and she decided to find a good one. If she could not find a job as fast as she hoped, then she would keep on trying. April decided that something good would come along. Anything was possible!

Page 6

B. 1. April made marks by the ads for jobs she thought she could do.

2. She was worn out from looking for a job.

3. She decided to paint the walls in her home.

4. Soon the walls would shine like new.

C. 1. worn 2. paint 3. walls 4. marks

D. April had a lot of hope as she looked for a job. But some nights she was worn out from looking. When she came back and saw the marks on her walls, she was upset. That's when she decided to paint the walls. "A good paint job is what I need," she said. She didn't know how long the old paint had been on the walls. She did know that new paint would make her home look good and make her feel good.

Page 7

B. 1. April's building was old.

2. Was it possible the color on the walls had once been gray?

3. April looked under the old paint to decide.

4. She asked the owner when painting had last been done.

C. 1. building 2. done 3. color 4. under

D. "Have you done this before?" asked Mr. Lopez, the building owner.

"I painted my home in my other building," said April. "I am fast and neat. I can do this in under four days."

"Well, you have picked a good color," said Mr. Lopez. "If you do a good job, I will give you back some money from your rent."

Page 8

A. lark, park, shark, spark

B. **1.** park **2.** bark **3.** mark **4.** dark

C. torn, scorn, sworn, thorn

D. **1.** torn **2.** worn, sworn **3.** born

Page 9

A. c<u>a</u>rd   f<u>ir</u>st   b<u>or</u>n   h<u>er</u>
n<u>ur</u>se   p<u>ar</u>t   th<u>ir</u>st   f<u>or</u>k
p<u>er</u>son   Th<u>ur</u>sday

B. card, hard, lard;
swirl, twirl, whirl;
fork, stork, York
curse, nurse, purse

C. **1.** p<u>er</u>son, h<u>ar</u>d **2.** f<u>ir</u>st, Th<u>ur</u>sday

3. Y<u>or</u>k **4.** n<u>ur</u>se

5. h<u>ar</u>d, p<u>ar</u>t

Page 12

<u>Think About It</u>

Discuss your answers with your instructor.

1. She was upset, a little surprised, and determined to get another job.

2. She had already painted three apartments.

3. She showed him photos of her work and told him that he could see the apartments in person.

4. Summaries should include: April lost her job and started looking for another one. In the meantime she painted her apartment and the apartments of some neighbors. She realized she liked painting, applied for a painting job, and got it.

<u>Write About It</u>

Discuss your writing with your instructor.

Page 13

1. F **2.** O **3.** O

4. F **5.** O **6.** F

7. O **8.** O

Page 14

A. **1.** April <u>needs</u> a new job.

2. <u>She</u> <u>talks</u> to the owner.

3. The <u>walls</u> <u>need</u> some paint.

4. Mr. Lopez <u>likes</u> April's work.

5. People <u>like</u> the color on the walls.

6. <u>They</u> <u>talk</u> about the colors.

B. **1.** ride

2. drive

3. hopes

4. marks

Page 15

C. **1.** <u>April</u> and <u>Mr. Baker</u> <u>talk</u> about the job.

2. The <u>wall</u> and the <u>door</u> <u>need</u> some paint.

3. The <u>boy</u> and his <u>mom</u> <u>help</u> April.

4. The <u>job</u> and the <u>work</u> <u>make</u> April happy.

5. <u>She</u> and her <u>family</u> <u>get</u> money this way.

6. The <u>job</u>, the <u>money</u>, and the <u>time</u> <u>seem</u> just fine.

D. **1.** make

2. need

3. help

4. look

5. like

Page 16

B. 1. #4, #11

2. a. Both ask for another skill as well as painting. Both jobs are in apartments.

b. #4 asks for experience, #11 doesn't. #4 asks for references, #11 doesn't.

3. #11 (It is his first job, so he doesn't have experience or references.)

C. Discuss your sentences with your instructor.

Unit 1 Review

Page 17

A. 1. building **2.** possible
3. decided **4.** business

B. 1. p<u>ark</u>, park **2.** w<u>orn</u>, worn
3. th<u>orn</u>, thorn **4.** sp<u>ark</u>, spark

C. 1. buses **2.** teaches **3.** bosses
4. boxes **5.** teaches **6.** boxes
7. bosses **8.** buses

Unit 2

Page 20

A. Answers will vary.

B. 1. Ray and his (wife) can't (spend) much money.

2. They need some (straight) talk about (cost).

3. Star is (pregnant), and she will be glad when she can (bring) the (baby) to see her parents.

4. The Popes need to shop with a good (company).

C. 1. table **2.** customer **3.** coupon **4.** save

Page 21

B. 1. The Popes needed <u>furniture</u>, <u>so</u> they went shopping.

2. They could not <u>afford</u> to spend much money.

3. They had saved a <u>little</u> money for <u>furniture</u>.

4. Many <u>furniture</u> sets cost <u>so</u> much that the Popes could not <u>afford</u> them.

5. They hoped to get the <u>furniture</u> and pay a <u>little</u> bit at a time.

C. 1. little
2. afford
3. so
4. furniture

D. Star and Ray wanted to forget about saving money when they saw the <u>furniture</u> they wanted. They liked it <u>so</u> much that they did not want to think about cost. But they could not <u>afford</u> all the <u>furniture</u> at once. Can they buy it a <u>little</u> at a time?

Page 22

B. 1. Star liked the pine set because it was <u>pretty</u>.

2. "Can a customer get <u>credit</u> here?" asked Star.

3. Mr. Silva, who worked in the store, took Ray's and Star's <u>names</u>.

4. Mr. Silva ran a <u>credit</u> <u>check</u> on them.

5. "I <u>checked</u> and your <u>credit</u> is <u>pretty</u> good," he told them.

C. 1. credit **2.** pretty **3.** check **4.** name

D. Ray and Star wanted to buy some <u>pretty</u> furniture before the baby came. They <u>checked</u> some ads to see about how much a bedroom set would cost. Ray and Star might have to buy the furniture on <u>credit</u>. They have a good <u>name</u> with <u>credit</u> companies because they pay bills on time.

Page 23

B. 1. "Will the bedroom set cost more if we pay <u>month</u> by <u>month</u>?" Star asked.

2. "<u>Yes</u>," said Ray. "It is <u>plain</u> that it will cost more if we buy on time."

3. "That is because you will be paying <u>interest</u> every <u>month</u>," Mr. Silva said.

C. 1. plain   2. month, month
3. Yes   4. interest

D. "Do you like this <u>plain</u> bedroom set?" Ray asked.

"<u>Yes</u>," Star said, "but I've been thinking of a pretty one for <u>months</u>."

Could they afford it? Ray and Star were trying to be responsible about money. They always used coupons when they shopped. They did not want to get into trouble over heavy <u>interest</u>.

Page 24

A. brain, chain, stain, strain

B. 1. stain   2. main   3. strain

C. blame, frame, shame

D. 1. shame 2. same   3. blame 4. came

Page 25

A. pl<u>ai</u>n   d<u>ay</u>   <u>age</u>   p<u>ai</u>n
p<u>ay</u>   n<u>a</u>m<u>e</u>   p<u>ai</u>d   pl<u>ay</u>
m<u>a</u>k<u>e</u>

B. maid, raid, braid;
way, stay, gray;
page, wage, stage;
drape, grape, shape

C. 1. sh<u>a</u>p<u>e</u>   2. dr<u>a</u>p<u>e</u>s   3. pl<u>ai</u>n
4. gr<u>ay</u>   5. w<u>ay</u>

Page 28

<u>Think About It</u>

Discuss your answers with your instructor.

1. They wanted to be sure they could afford it. They didn't like the fast talk they were getting from the salesman.

2. They didn't feel he was giving them answers to their questions.

3. They found it two months later.

4. Summaries should include: Ray and Star went looking for a bedroom set. The first set they saw was expensive and the salesman didn't have credit terms they could afford. Ray and Star kept looking and then bought a bedroom set at another store.

<u>Write About It</u>

Discuss your writing with your instructor.

Page 29

1. Both furniture stores have credit plans.

2. One offers a better interest rate than the other.

3. They both have credit plans.   Both

4. One has a better interest rate.   However

Page 30

A. 1. older, oldest

2. straighter, straightest

3. neater, neatest

4. longer, longest

5. tighter, tightest

6. cleaner, cleanest

B. "This is a long table, but I want a <u>longer</u> one," said Ray. "My sister has the <u>longest</u> table in the family. We can all sit at that table."

"Our <u>older</u> table will have to do for now. Our money will be <u>tighter</u> when we buy a bedroom set," said Star.

C. 1. cleanest 2. smaller 3. longest

Page 31

D. 1. smaller 2. older 3. longer

E. 1. smallest 2. longest 3. oldest

F. Discuss your sentences with your instructor.

Page 32

B. 1. **a.** $1,086.04 **b.** $286.04

2. **a.** 9-8-01 **b.** $63.00 **c.** $15.04

3. 21%

Unit 2 Review

Page 33

A. 1. interest 2. afford

3. credit 4. month

B. 1. sh<u>a</u>me, shame 2. bl<u>a</u>me, blame

3. m<u>ai</u>n, main 4. str<u>ai</u>n, strain

C. 1. smallest 2. newer

3. finest 4. cleaner

Unit 3

Page 36

A. Answers will vary

B. 1. The (players) come from (different) (countries.)

2. They (enjoy) working (together) to make a new kind of music.

3. The (group) has many (fans) who buy their (records.)

4. Wherever they play, (people) come to (listen.)

C. 1. listen 2. tune *or* records

3. enjoy 4. countries

Page 37

B. 1. They had once been <u>popular</u> <u>musicians</u>.

2. Ry Cooder heard their <u>songs</u> on old records.

3. He thought it would be a shame if their music <u>died</u>.

4. Now their <u>songs</u> are <u>popular</u> in many countries.

C. 1. musicians

2. songs

3. popular

4. died

D. Music from other countries has become <u>popular</u>. People in Canada sing <u>songs</u> from Africa and people in Japan hum tunes from Finland. <u>Musicians</u> bring new ideas to old ways of playing and singing. Many types of music that might have <u>died</u> out have found new life.

Page 38

B. **1.** <u>World</u> music begins with the <u>style</u> of a particular place.

2. Players use new <u>instruments</u> to play old music.

3. They combine their music with <u>styles</u> from different parts of the <u>world</u>.

4. When they are ready, they play <u>live</u> for hundreds of people.

C. **1.** live, world

2. style

3. instruments

4. live

D. The musicians travel all over the <u>world</u> to play <u>live</u> for their fans. Everywhere they go they learn about new <u>styles</u> of music. They see strange <u>instruments</u>. They use some of these new <u>styles</u> and <u>instruments</u> in their own music.

Page 39

B. **1.** Her songs have beautiful <u>melodies</u>.

2. Songs with fast <u>rhythms</u> make me want to dance.

3. The guitar <u>combines</u> with other instruments to make a lovely sound.

4. Sad music is a part of their <u>tradition</u>.

C. **1.** rhythms

2. tradition

3. combine

4. melodies

D. When people came to America from Ireland, they brought their musical <u>tradition</u> with them. In the new country, Irish music <u>combined</u> with other <u>traditions</u>. You can still hear Irish <u>rhythms</u> and <u>melodies</u> in many American popular songs.

Page 40

A. lie, tie

B. **1.** die   **2.** tie   **3.** lie

C. rice, slice, twice, splice

D. **1.** twice   **2.** nice   **3.** price

Page 41

A. d<u>ie</u>, r<u>ice</u>, r<u>igh</u>t, f<u>i</u>nd, wh<u>y</u>; t<u>ie</u>, f<u>i</u>ve, h<u>igh</u>, ch<u>i</u>ld, tr<u>y</u>

B. drive, live, thrive; bright, fright, plight; mind, wind, blind; dry, sky, fly

C. **1.** h<u>igh</u>, pr<u>ice</u>

2. m<u>i</u>nd

3. fl<u>y</u>

4. thr<u>ive</u>

5. dr<u>ive</u>

Page 44

<u>Think About It</u>

1. World music combines the traditional music of particular places with the rhythms and instruments from other places to create a new style of music.

2. Värttinä's home country is Finland.

3. Papa Wemba helped create soukous music.

4. Benin is in Africa.

<u>Write About It</u>

Discuss your writing with your instructor.

Page 45

A. 2,1,3

B. **1. c.** after Ry Cooder found the old Cuban musicians.

2. c. when Papa Wemba added electric instruments.

3. b. before she became famous.

Page 46

A. **1.** June 18, 2000

2. It goes between the day and the year (June 18, 2000).

3. Dear

4. He offers to pick Sam up, give him a place to stay, and a ticket.

5. Your friend, Ned

B. Discuss the letter with your instructor.

Page 47

C. **1.** Ned Dean
in the upper left hand corner
the return address

2. Sam Best
in the center of the envelope
the mailing address

3.–5. Ned Dean
407 New St.
Compton, NY 12433

Sam Best
1219 Center Street
Packway, CT 06008

D. Discuss the envelope with your instructor.

Page 48

A. N, S, E, W

B. **1.** north **2.** west

3. south **4.** east

5. west **6.** north

Unit 3 Review

Page 49

A. **1.** songs, musicians, melodies, *or* rhythms

2. world

3. popular

4. style *or* rhythms

B. **1.** tw*ice*, twice

2. d*ie*, die

3. pr*ice*, price

4. l*ie*, lie

C. Discuss the parts of your letter with your instructor.

Unit 4

Page 52

A. Answers will vary.

B. **1.** Some mean kids live around here.

2. I never come home late from a party or movie.

3. Every person who lives here could help make this a safer place.

C. **1.** club **2.** always

3. once **4.** party

5. late **6.** kids

7. mean

Page 53

B. 1. It isn't <u>very</u> safe for kids to play here.

2. A <u>guard</u> could help to <u>protect</u> the kids.

3. We asked the owners of the building to help us <u>protect</u> our homes.

4. They were <u>very</u> nice but didn't <u>show</u> much interest in our problems.

C. 1. guards   2. very

3. show   4. protect

D.   Zack, a small child who lives in 10A, had a <u>very</u> bad time this month. Some mean kids came into the building. They asked Zack to <u>show</u> them his video games. He got <u>very</u> upset and ran away from them. His family is new in the building, so he didn't know who could <u>protect</u> him.

    Zack is OK now, but his mother is still <u>very</u> upset. She wants to get some <u>guards</u> in the building to help <u>protect</u> Zack and all the other little kids.

Page 54

B. 1. We can't let <u>any</u> <u>strangers</u> come into the building.

2. Some of them make trouble on the <u>grounds</u>.

3. I tell my kids not to talk to <u>any</u> <u>strangers</u>.

4. We need a guard to <u>watch</u> the <u>grounds</u>.

5. A guard won't let <u>strangers</u> onto the <u>grounds</u>.

C. 1. strangers   2. watch

3. any   4. grounds

D.   Some <u>strangers</u> are very friendly, but at our building we can't take <u>any</u> chances. I was coming home late one night after a party. I wasn't <u>watching</u> when some <u>strangers</u> came into the building <u>grounds</u> after me. I didn't know <u>any</u> of them and didn't know if they lived here. I found my key and went in. Then they came after me and hit me. I yelled for help. I was lucky that Mr. Price, the <u>guard</u>, was around. The men were arrested. Later, I told Mr. Price how glad I am that he is here on the <u>grounds</u>.

Page 55

B. 1. This <u>kind</u> of building is like a small <u>town</u>.

2. Still, I <u>worry</u> when my kids go out <u>alone</u>.

3. I <u>worry</u> that I cannot watch them all the time.

4. Not all strangers will be <u>kind</u> to children.

5. Ming must learn to get around <u>town</u> <u>alone</u>.

C. 1. kind   2. worry   3. alone   4. town

D.   I cannot keep my job and still be with my kids all the time. If we lived in a small <u>town</u> or in the country, maybe I could do it. But here, in this building in a big city, it's not safe for the kids to be <u>alone</u>. I <u>worry</u> because I've had problems and want to keep my kids from having the same <u>kind</u> of trouble.

Page 56

A. hound   mound   sound   rounds

B. 1. around   2. rounds   3. sound

C. brown   drown   frown   clown

D. 1. frown   2. brown   3. town

Page 57

A. 1. f<u>ou</u>nd   m<u>ou</u>nd   p<u>ou</u>nd   <u>ou</u>t

     2. t<u>ow</u>n   br<u>ow</u>n   cl<u>ow</u>n   h<u>ow</u>

B. sh<u>ou</u>t   v<u>ow</u>   spr<u>ou</u>t   br<u>ow</u>

C. sh<u>ou</u>t   p<u>ou</u>nd   gr<u>ou</u>p   c<u>ou</u>pon

     m<u>ou</u>nd   w<u>ou</u>nd   s<u>ou</u>p

D. h<u>ow</u>   br<u>ow</u>n   sh<u>ow</u>   <u>ow</u>n

     fr<u>ow</u>n   g<u>ow</u>n   gr<u>ow</u>   kn<u>ow</u>n

E. 1. gr<u>ow</u>   2. v<u>ow</u>   3. <u>ow</u>n

Page 60

Think About It

Discuss your answers with your instructor.

1. The building where she lived wasn't safe.

2. They organized, held meetings, made a list of safety tips, and presented a strong case to the owners.

3. It was much safer—more guards, gates locked at night, cooperation with city cops, kids more aware of safety rules.

4. Summaries should include: Kim worried about her children being safe where they lived because there had been several incidents. She organized neighbors, and they got the building owners to improve safety conditions.

Write About It

Discuss your writing with your instructor.

Page 61

B. 1. People from another apartment building came to see Kim.

     2. They wanted to know what was being done there to protect occupants.

     3. They wanted to make their building safe.

C. 2. Kim's work had helped to make her building safer.

Page 62

A. 1. cries   2. babies   3. worried

     4. carried   5. pries

B. 1. line to partied   2. line to babies

     3. line to fried   4. line to carries

     5. line to tried

C.   Lan <u>cries</u> when I tell her not to go out alone. Ming says that I have <u>babied</u> her too much. Time <u>flies</u> and she is getting older, but I still worry. Once, she couldn't find her way home. How I <u>worried</u> then! Now Lan belongs to a club and plays with kids her own age.

Page 63

D. 1. tries

     2. cried

     3. carried

     4. worries

E. 1. cries, cried   2. spies, spied

     3. babies, babied   4. worries, worried

     5. carries, carried

F. Discuss your sentences with your instructor.

Page 64

B. **1.** My parents can't come to the phone now. What is your name and number?

2. When children call for help, they can quickly tell someone how to find them.

Unit 4 Review

Page 65

A. **1.** worry   **2.** alone
    3. grounds   **4.** guard

B. **1.** t<u>own</u>, town   **2.** ar<u>ound</u>, around
    3. f<u>ound</u>, found   **4.** d<u>own</u>, down

C. **1.** carries   **2.** worries
    3. cried   **4.** tried

Unit 5

Page 68

B. **1.** Rocky was down (because) he was not doing well in (school.)

2. Carla worried that he had lost (interest) in (ninth) grade.

3. Carla had her own (problems) to (cope) with at work.

C. **1.** always   **2.** desk   **3.** wrong
    4. knew   **5.** slowly   **6.** listen

Page 69

B. **1.** Many people have seemed to be <u>failures</u> in school work.

2. Lots of <u>those</u> people go on to do very well.

3. It is hard to feel <u>joy</u> if you feel like a <u>failure</u>.

4. Most schools have <u>programs</u> for <u>those</u> who need help.

C. **1.** program   **2.** joy   **3.** failure   **4.** those

D. One night Carla and Rocky watched a <u>program</u> together on TV. It was about people who seemed to be <u>failures</u> but went on to do very well. Some of <u>those</u> people were popular musicians. Others had top careers as writers, senators, doctors, and business leaders. "Anything is possible," thought Carla as she watched the <u>program</u>. She could tell from the <u>joy</u> in his eyes that Rocky had this feeling, too.

Page 70

B. **1.** No one <u>really</u> wants to be a failure.

2. Some people <u>just</u> take longer to find their way.

3. <u>Success</u> means different things to different people.

4. Some people who wear leg <u>braces</u> learn to be top runners.

5. A bad outlook can <u>really</u> <u>spoil</u> your chances of <u>success</u>.

C. **1.** success
    2. spoil
    3. really
    4. just
    5. brace

D. Carla and Rocky were <u>really</u> interested to learn about all the <u>successful</u> people who had had problems. These people didn't let their problems <u>spoil</u> things for them. They <u>just</u> kept trying. One man became a big <u>success</u> as a stockbroker. He made a lot of money. Reading was <u>just</u> harder for him than for some people. Other people who wore leg <u>braces</u> went on to become top sports stars.

Page 71

B. 1. Carla does not buy many things on impulse.

2. She wanted to order this video for Rocky.

3. The video might have some answers for him.

4. It would show him that many famous people had problems before they found success.

C. 1. answer

2. order

3. impulse

4. famous

D. On an impulse Carla checked with the video company to see how soon her order would be sent. She got an answer right away. Her order for the "Famous Failures" video was in the mail. Carla told Rocky about her impulse order. His answer gave her hope.

"The TV show about famous people with problems was interesting," he said. "So maybe the video will be, too. It was a good impulse, Mom. I'm glad you ordered that video."

Page 72

A. coil, foil, toil, broil

B. 1. toil   2. spoil *or* foil   3. boil

C. joy, soy, toy

D. 1. joy   2. boy   3. toy

Page 73

A. oil, spoil, choice, oily, join, noise, ointment, point, hoist, coin, poison

B. oyster, joy, boycott, boy, annoy, employ, loyal, toy, disloyal, voyage, ahoy, joyful

C. 1. annoy   2. point   3. spoil
4. employ   5. choices

Page 76

Think About It

1. He had problems with his reading and felt like a failure.

2. She bought a video about famous people who overcame problems to achieve success.

3. He felt empowered and encouraged.

4. Rocky, a ninth grader, has reading problems and feels like a failure in school. He wants to quit. His mother orders a video about famous people who overcome various problems to go on to success. Rocky is inspired by the video and does a report for school on some of the people.

Write About It

Discuss your writing with your instructor.

Page 77

B. 1. She should consider the importance of learning this part of her job. She should be encouraged because she has learned new things before.

2. Answers will vary. Students might say that Carla should discuss the problem with her boss and work with him to figure out a way for her to learn the new assignment.

Page 78

A. 1. singular   2. plural

   3. singular   4. plural

B.   <u>Rocky's</u> interest in reading problems led him to set up a web site. He likes to read the <u>visitors'</u> e-mails. Many <u>women's</u> letters ask about <u>Rocky's</u> mother. Some of the letters tell about a <u>kid's</u> reading success or a <u>school's</u> reading program. Other <u>writers'</u> e-mails ask about the <u>video's</u> stories.

C. 1. learners'   2. parents'   3. runners'

   4. helpers'   5. sisters'

Page 79

D. 1. Carla's son

   2. many strangers' letters

   3. the radio's program

   4. both legs' braces

   5. three boys' homework

E. 1. This <u>book's</u> words are hard, but those <u>books'</u> words are not.

   2. Too many failures can add to a <u>kid's</u> troubles.

   3. The <u>girl's</u> successes came from her <u>father's</u> help.

F. Discuss your sentences with your instructor.

Page 80

B. 1. There were no women doctors and the medical schools rejected her.

   2. Winston Churchill failed the sixth grade.

   3. He became one of the world's most famous scientists.

   4. He was a world famous painter.

   5. Answers will vary, but should include the reason.

Unit 5 Review

Page 81

A. 1. success   2. failure

   3. programs   4. hard

B. 1. j<u>oy</u>, joy   2. sp<u>oi</u>l, spoil

   3. s<u>oi</u>l, soil   4. t<u>oy</u>, toy

C. 1. Rocky's   2. programs'

   3. boys'   4. mothers'

Unit 6

Page 84

A. Answers will vary.

B. 1. Pam stopped (sweeping) and (cooking) for a minute.

   2. (Then) she (picked) up the card from Rose.

   3. The last (sentence) said, "I've got the (blues) because I've (been) (thinking) of you."

   4. Pam would be so glad (if) Rose could come to see her (before) this (year) is over.

C.

		¹h		
²b	e	f	o	r	e
		r		
	³t	h	e	n

Page 85

B. 1. I know about the <u>immigration</u> laws here.

   2. It took me a long time to get my own <u>green</u> card.

   3. Rose doesn't need <u>permission</u> to <u>visit</u> me.

   4. If Rose wanted to work here, she would have to get a <u>green</u> card.

5. The immigration laws try to keep newcomers from taking work that people here could do.

C. 1. green   2. visit

    3. permission   4. immigration

D.   When I first wanted to come to this country, I didn't know much about the immigration laws. I waited to get my green card so I would have permission to work for the Prices. Getting a green card is much harder than coming here to visit.

Page 86

B. 1. I keep house for my American employers.

    2. I do the best I can with their house and the children.

    3. The Prices gave me a responsible job and a small room in their house.

    4. Some of the money I make goes to help my family back home.

C. 1. goes   2. American

    3. house   4. employers

D.   The American immigration laws say I must have a green card to work in this country. Not many Americans want to be a housekeeper, so this kind of job goes to people like me. I'm lucky because the Prices are good employers.

Page 87

B. 1. I needed legal help to get a green card.

    2. Getting a green card takes time, money, and many calls, letters, and legal papers.

    3. I had to draw money out of my savings to pay for the legal costs.

    4. The immigration people checked to see that the legal papers were right.

C. 1. legal   2. papers   3. draw   4. called

D.   Every day when Ike and Shelly come home from school, they call their mother at her job. Then they show me their drawings and school papers. We laugh and kid around. This draws my thoughts away from Rose and my island home. It's nice not to have legal papers to worry about anymore.

Page 88

A. tall, wall, small

B. 1. call   2. tall *or* small   3. small

C. paw   flaw   draw   straw

D. 1. law   2. draw   3. flaw

Page 89

B. parent–2   credit–2
    responsible–4   newcomer–3
    arrested–3   strain–1

D. about–a   sentence–e   doctor–o
    April–i   actor–o   August–u

E. 1. another 2. Americans 3. papers

Page 92

<u>Think About It</u>

1. She missed her sister and her island home.

2. She introduced Rose to the Browns who wanted Rose to work for them.

3. Summaries should include: Pam wrote to her sister Rose. Rose visited Pam in the United States and wanted to come here to work. Mrs. Brown got pregnant and sponsored Rose to come here as a babysitter.

<u>Write About It</u>

Discuss your writing with your instructor.

Page 93

1. b　　**2.** a　　**3.** b　　**4.** c

Page 94

B.　　Rose <u>wrote</u> to Pam. Rose <u>told</u> about the legal work she <u>was</u> doing to get her green card. She <u>brought</u> her problems to a woman who <u>drew</u> up the papers she <u>needed</u>. Rose <u>knew</u> it would take a long time to get the green card. She <u>fought</u> hard not to get upset or give up trying.

C.　**1.** ate　　**2.** swept　　**3.** swam

Page 95

D.　**1.** keep　**2.** know　**3.** fought　**4.** swim

　　5. drive　**6.** ate　**7.** brought　**8.** sweep

E.　**1.** Rose wrote about her green card.

　　2. Pam knew the Brown family.

　　3. Mrs. Brown drove Pam to the store.

F.　Discuss your sentences with your instructor.

Page 96

B.　**1.** first name　　**2.** line 3

　　3. female　　**4.** line 6

Unit 6 Review

Page 97

A.　**1.** immigration　**2.** visit

　　3. permission　　**4.** green

B.　**1.** saw, saw　　**2.** small, small

　　3. call, call　　**4.** law, law

C.　**1.** wrote　　**2.** kept

　　3. fought　　**4.** knew

Unit 7

Page 100

A.　Answers will vary.

B.　**1.** Pedro saw someone at the card shop he would like to know better.

　　2. How would he talk to someone who was so pretty?

　　3. Why was he too shy to ask her for a date?

C.

s	u	m	m	e	r
o		u			
o		s			
n		t	h	a	n	k

Page 101

B. 1. Pedro <u>noticed</u> the <u>girl</u> right away.

2. Seeing her for the first time gave him a <u>start</u>.

3. She was too good to be <u>true</u>!

4. Pedro didn't know if the <u>girl</u> <u>noticed</u> him.

5. He wanted to say something, but he didn't know where to <u>start</u>.

C. 1. started 2. girl 3. notice 4. true

D.   Pedro couldn't get the <u>girl</u> from the card shop out of his mind. He <u>started</u> thinking about how he could meet her. He would go back to the shop and get her to <u>notice</u> him. It was <u>true</u> that he didn't need more cards, but he would go back to the shop anyway.

Page 102

B. 1. Pedro's <u>idea</u> was to go back to the shop soon.

2. He would look at the <u>birthday</u> cards this time.

3. The shop was <u>open</u>, but only a <u>few</u> people were there.

4. Pedro had no <u>idea</u> what to say to the girl.

C. 1. few 2. ideas 3. birthday 4. open

D.   Pedro <u>opened</u> one card after another. Soon he would have to buy a <u>few</u>. The girl would get the wrong <u>idea</u> if he didn't buy some, so he picked out a <u>few</u> <u>birthday</u> cards and went to her. When he tried to pay her, he dropped his money. The girl didn't say anything, but Pedro got the <u>idea</u> that she must be laughing at him.

Page 103

B. 1. Pedro <u>wished</u> to talk to the girl, but he was shy.

2. "<u>Please</u> tell me your name," he asked.

3. He learned that her name was Ana, but still he was <u>far</u> from asking her out.

4. "<u>Please</u> tell me why you buy so many cards," she said.

5. Pedro started to feel <u>warm</u> all over and forgot what he wanted to say.

C. 1. wished 2. warmly

3. pleased 4. far

D.   Pedro wasn't too <u>pleased</u> about buying so many cards. "I <u>wish</u> I could think of another way to see Ana," he thought. "She doesn't know me, so I won't get too <u>far</u> if I just ask her out. I <u>wish</u> I could get her to <u>warm</u> up to the <u>idea</u> of a date."

Page 104

A. clue, flue, glue

B. 1. true 2. blue 3. clue 4. due

C. chew, flew, crew, threw

D. 1. grew 2. few 3. threw 4. new

Page 105

A. f<u>oo</u>d   bl<u>ue</u>   bl<u>ew</u>   gr<u>ou</u>p

   m<u>oo</u>d   cl<u>ue</u>   ch<u>ew</u>   s<u>ou</u>p

B. moon   cool   noon

   pool   swoon   stool

C. g<u>oo</u>d   h<u>oo</u>d   c<u>ou</u>ld   sh<u>ou</u>ld

   w<u>oo</u>d   st<u>oo</u>d   w<u>ou</u>ld

D. book   brook   cook

   crook   hook   shook

E. 1. cool 2. shook

Page 108

Discuss your answers with your instructor.

1. He was shy.

2. He bought many cards and finally gave her one.

3. They became friends and started going out.

4. Summaries should include: Pedro saw Ana working in a card shop and really liked her. He went often to the shop and bought cards so that he could see her. He was too shy to ask her out. He gave her a card, they talked, and they decided to go out together.

Write About It

Discuss your writing with your instructor.

Page 109

B. 2. Get-Well Cards and Birthday Cards

C.

Get-Well	Birthday
three cards	dogs
nurse	flags
two had cats	kites

Page 110

A. 1. himself   **2.** herself

  3. yourself   **4.** myself

B. 1. yourselves   **2.** themselves

  3. ourselves

C. 1. yourself   **2.** themselves

  3. ourselves   **4.** herself

  5. myself

Page 111

D. On Monday Ana was by <u>herself</u> in the store. "There are not so many customers now, so I can work by <u>myself</u>," she said. "Most people help <u>themselves</u> when it comes to buying cards."

On Tuesday Pedro came in by <u>himself</u>. He looked at the cards by <u>himself</u> for a long time. When he brought a card for Ana to ring up, she said, "You bought <u>yourself</u> a good card. I like that one."

Pedro's eyes lit up. "Thanks!" he said. As he opened the door, he turned and said, "Take care of <u>yourself</u> now."

E. 1. <u>yourselves</u>; "We can open up the shop ourselves," Ana told her helper.

  2. <u>herself</u>; Ana said, "I, myself, need to write some checks."

  3. <u>themselves</u>; A customer talked to himself as he picked out a card.

F. Discuss your sentences with your instructor.

Page 112

B. 1. a. a dinner salad or any of the extras

    b. shrimp

  2. Beverages

  3. Answers will vary. The total cost of the lunch must be $6.00 or less.

Unit 7 Review

Page 113

A. 1. idea   **2.** wished

  3. please   **4.** noticed

B. 1. bl<u>ue</u>, blue   **2.** cl<u>ue</u>, clue

  3. n<u>ew</u>, new   **4.** gr<u>ew</u>, grew

C. 1. himself   **2.** herself

  3. yourself   **4.** myself

135

Final Review

Pages 114–117

A. 1. building

2. furniture, worn

3. possible, business

4. decided

5. afford

6. credit, check

B. 1. ark   park   park

2. ain   strain   strain

3. ice   nice   nice

4. ive   five   five

C.

<u>Food</u>	<u>Homes</u>	<u>Clothes</u>
meat	house	pants
rice	apartment	socks
milk	hut	hat

D. 1. worries

2. mother's

3. cried

4. brothers'

E. 1. smallest

2. cleanest

3. neater

F. 1. popular, town

2. musician

3. instrument

4. show

5. any

6. styles

G. 1. own   town   town

2. oil   spoil   spoil

3. ound   around   around

4. oy   toy   toy

5. oy   joy   joy

6. ound   found   found

H. 1. employer

2. success

3. noticed

4. famous

5. American

6. true

7. please

8. idea

I. 1. wrote

2. kept

3. fought

4. knew

J. 1. ew   new   new

2. all   hall   hall

3. aw   saw   saw

4. ue   blue   blue

K. 1. herself

2. myself

3. yourself

4. ourselves

Word List

Below is a list of the 302 words that are presented to students in *Book Five* of *Reading for Today*. These words are introduced on sight word, phonics, and language pages. The words will be reviewed in later books. Students should also be familiar with other words based on the phonetically regular spellings of long and short vowel sounds in the consonant-vowel-consonant (CVC) and consonant-vowel-consonant + silent *e* (CVC + *e*) patterns.

A
address
afford
ahoy
alone
American
annoy
answer
any
apartments
ate

B
babied
bark
beverages
birthday
blame
blew
blind
blue
boil
book
born
bosses
box
boxes
boy
boycott
brace
braid
brain
bright
broil
brook
brought
brow
brown
building

buses
business

C
call
carried
carries
chain
check
chew
choice
cleaner
cleanest
clown
clue
coil
coin
color
combine
cook
cool
coy
credit
crew
cried
crook
crown
curse

D
dark
decided
dice
die
died
disloyal
done
drape
draw
drew

drove
drown
due

E
east
emergency
employ
employer
experienced
extras

F
failure
fall
famous
far
fast
female
few
fix
fixes
flaw
flew
flue
foil
fork
form
fought
frame
fright
frown
furniture

G
gain
girl
glue
goes
grape

grasses
green
grew
grounds
grow
guard

H
herself
high
himself
hoist
hook
horn
hound
hour
house

I
idea
immigration
impulse
information
instruments
insurance
interest

J
jaw
joy
joyful
just

K
kept
kind
knew

L
lark
least

legal
library
lie
little
live
longest
loyal

M
maid
main
male
marks
melodies
menu
middle
minute
month
mood
moon
mound
musicians
myself

N
name
neater
neatest
nice
noise
noon
north
noticed
number

O
oil
oily
ointment
older

oldest
open
order
ourselves
oyster

P
page
pain
paint
papers
part
paw
payment
permission
pie
plain
please
plight
point
poison
pool
popular
possible
pound
pretty
programs
protect
purse

R
raid
rain
really
references
rhythm
rice
river
rounds

S

same
saw
scorn
shame
shape
shark
shook
shout
show
slice
smaller
smallest
so
soil
songs
sound
soup
south
soy
spark
special
spied
spies
splice
spoil
sprout
stage
stain
start
stood
stool
straighter
straightest
strain
strangers
style
success
straw
swam
swept
swirl
swoon
sworn

T

tall
teaches
telephone
their
themselves
thirst
thorn
those
threw
thrive
tie
tighter
tightest
toil
torn
total
town
toy
tradition
tried
tries
true
twice
twirl

U

under

V

very
vie
visit
vow
voyage

W

wage
wait
walls
warm
warranty
watch
watches
west

whirl
wind
wish
wishes
wood
world
worn
worried
worries
worry
wrote

Y

yes
York
yourself
yourselves

Skill	Completion	Skill	Completion	Skill	Completion

Unit 1

Review Words............................☐
Sight Words ....☐
Phonics: *-ark* and *-orn* ....☐
Phonics: Vowels with *-r*...............☐
Comprehension: Think
   and Write.............................☐
Comprehension Skills: Fact
   and Opinion ....☐
Writing Skills: Subject-Verb
   Agreement...........................☐
Life Skills: Reading Help
   Wanted Ads.........................☐
Unit 1 Review ....☐

Unit 2

Review Words............................☐
Sight Words ....☐
Phonics: *-ain* and *-ame* ....☐
Phonics: Long *a*.......................☐
Comprehension: Think
   and Write.............................☐
Comprehension Skills:
   Comparing and Contrasting.☐
Writing Skills: Comparisons........☐
Life Skills: Reading a Payment
   Schedule ....☐
Unit 2 Review ....☐

Unit 3

Review Words............................☐
Sight Words ....☐
Phonics: *-ie* and *-ice* ....☐
Phonics: Long *i*.......................☐
Comprehension: Think
   and Write.............................☐

Comprehension Skills:
   Sequence ....☐
Writing Skills: Writing a
   Friendly Letter....................☐
Life Skills: Reading a Map ....☐
Unit 3 Review ....☐

Unit 4

Review Words............................☐
Sight Words ....☐
Phonics: *-ound* and *-own* ....☐
Phonics: *-ou* and *-ow* ....☐
Comprehension: Think
   and Write.............................☐
Comprehension Skills:
   Inference ....☐
Writing Skills: Adding Endings
   to *-y* Words...........................☐
Life Skills: Telephone Safety........☐
Unit 4 Review ....☐

Unit 5

Review Words............................☐
Sight Words ....☐
Phonics: *-oil* and *-oy* ....☐
Phonics: *-oi* and *-oy*....................☐
Comprehension: Think
   and Write.............................☐
Comprehension Skills: Making
   Judgments ....☐
Writing Skills: Plural Possessive
   Nouns..................................☐
Life Skills: Reading a Chart ....☐
Unit 5 Review ....☐

Unit 6

Review Words............................☐
Sight Words ....☐
Phonics: *-all* and *-aw*..............☐
Phonics: Syllables and Schwa .....☐
Comprehension: Think
   and Write.............................☐
Comprehension Skills:
   Drawing Conclusions.............☐
Writing Skills: Irregular Verbs .....☐
Life Skills: Filling Out a Form .....☐
Unit 6 Review ....☐

Unit 7

Review Words............................☐
Sight Words ....☐
Phonics: *-ue* and *-ew*...................☐
Phonics: $\bar{oo}$ and $\breve{oo}$ ....☐
Comprehension: Think
   and Write.............................☐
Comprehension Skills:
   Classifying...........................☐
Writing Skills: Reflexive
   Pronouns ....☐
Life Skills: Reading a Menu ....☐
Unit 7 Review ....☐

Final Review................................☐